Time Began in a Garden

NARRATIVE BY
Emilie Barnes
WITH
Anne Christian Buchanan

PAINTINGS BY
Glynda Turley

HARVEST HOUSE PUBLISHERS
Eugene, Oregon 97402

OTHER BOOKS BY EMILIE BARNES

The Spirit of Loveliness
15 Minute Family Traditions and Memories
The Creative Home Organizer
Eating Right
The 15-Minute Organizer
More Hours in My Day
My Prayer Planner
Survival for Busy Women
Things Happen When Women Care
15 Minutes Alone with God
The 15-Minute Money Manager
The Daily Planner
If Teacups Could Talk

To obtain additional information about Emilie Barnes' seminars and tapes send a self-addressed, stamped business envelope to:

MORE HOURS IN MY DAY
2838 Rumsey Drive
Riverside, CA 92506

Art direction, design, and production by
Garborg Design Works, Minneapolis, Minnesota

TIME BEGAN IN A GARDEN

Copyright © 1995 by Harvest House Publishers
Eugene, Oregon 97402

Library of Congress Cataloging-in-Publication Data

Barnes, Emilie.
   Time Began in a Garden / Emilie Barnes with Anne Christian Buchanan :
      paintings by Glynda Turley
         p.   cm.
      ISBN 1-56507-368-1
      1. Gardening. 2. Barnes, Emilie. 3. Nature craft. 4. Gardening—Religious aspects—Christianity.
   I. Buchanan, Anne Christian. II. Title
      SB455.B282 1995
      635.9—dc20   95-12630
                                                                                          CIP

Selected recipes are taken from *The Eating Better Cookbooks,* ©1994 by Rich and Sue Gregg, 8830 Glencoe Drive, Riverside, CA 92503.

With deep love,
appreciation, and
devotion, I dedicate this
book to my beloved
husband,
Bob,
who at our first
meeting over forty years
ago brought me a
flower from the garden
and has ever since.
My Bob is really the
gardener in our family
and has the touch of
not only a green thumb
but also of a whole
being that reflects
love and beauty into
my life.

CONTENTS

Where Time Begins Again

It may be true that time began in a garden.

But not the ticking, tocking, got-to-get-it-done-no-matter-what kind of time.

Not the stuffed, crammed Daytimer kind of time—the sorry-I'm-late-I-got-stuck-on-the-freeway form of measurement.

The time that began in a garden is the kind of time I go to our garden to find again.

It's time the way God created it: as a servant and not a master.

This kind of time is a container for worthwhile work, a resource for creating the beautiful and feeding the hungry and growing the soul. It is measured in drifting or purposeful hours, in day and then night and then day again, in slowly rolling seasons, each with its special purpose under heaven.

Garden time is time that involves itself in the moment, that passes each moment fully alive, that focuses on the soaring stateliness of trees and the minute scale of the tiniest blossom and insect. Garden time requires daily attention but does not require that everything be done in a day.

I go to my garden to rediscover that kind of time. And I have to take time out from the other kind of time to discover it.

Why don't you take time out, too?

Come away from your rat race, your conveyor belt, your traffic jam, to be renewed and refreshed in the company of growing things.

It won't take long, but it will feel like a day in the country.

You're on garden time now.

"Just living is not enough," said the butterfly.
"One must have sunshine, freedom, and a little flower."
Hans Christian Andersen

A Time for Re-Creation

Why I Need a Garden in My Life

The very first garden I remember was a sweet potato in a jar.

My mama planted it when we were living in three tiny rooms behind our dress shop. There was no yard, no room outside for even a flowerpot. But Mama filled a Mason jar with water, propped the long, skinny sweet potato up in the glass with a trio of toothpicks, and told my brother and me to watch.

By summer, the kitchen window was curtained with graceful vines and big, curving leaves. And somehow that window garden made our shabby little kitchen into a special place. Even the light seemed different—more restful, more alive.

That was when I first realized I needed a garden in my life. I needed that different light, that tender green beauty, that sense of companionship with growing things.

And flowers! I needed flowers the way I needed food. Sometimes we would walk home from the streetcar past concrete-embedded trees and little beds of public pansies. Mama would always pick a few to float in a bowl or gather in a jelly jar.

Sometimes we would splurge and spend precious money on daisies or carnations from a florist. Those modest bouquets always added cheer and grace far out of proportion to the financial sacrifice.

Later, during a painful time when my poor, overworked mother was unable to make a home for us, I went to live with my Auntie Evelyn. And there I was bitten in earnest by the gardening bug. How I loved to walk with her among her beautiful roses, learning how to cut and gather and arrange lovely bouquets, taking to heart the reality that a little patch of soil and some loving attention could create an uncommon amount of beauty and joy.

Not too long after that I met and married my Bob. And while I didn't marry him for his green thumb, I'm sure that our mutual love of growing things helped bring us together—or helped keep us together. From the time we moved into our first tiny apartment, we have managed to maintain a garden of some kind: from a collection of potted geraniums on an apartment table to our current acre and a half with its fish pond and fruit trees and rose arbor and lush raised beds for vegetables.

> More than anything, I must have flowers, always, always.
> CLAUDE MONET

Although I have consistently been involved with what was happening in our yards, I've always said that Bob was the real gardener. But I don't say that anymore. For I've learned that there are as many kinds of gardens as there are gardeners. All of them are "real." Our lives are inevitably richer for whatever efforts we exert toward making plants a part of our lives.

There are gardeners who love nothing better than wrestling with the elements: digging bare fingers deep in the soil, struggling with shovels, digging and redigging and planting and replanting, making and remaking their gardens as they strive toward the dream in their mind. They are the artists and the engineers of the garden; they thrive on the challenge of turning bare ground into something lovely and fruitful.

Other gardeners are the nurturers, who love to attend to growing things the way they attend to children. These men and women find a parent's joy in tucking the tiny seeds into beds and watching the tender shoots grow taller.

And then there are the impatient gardeners—more and more common in these hectic days—who love to buy their plants ready-grown and already blooming. For them, gardening is less a matter of digging and sowing than of grouping little pots in bigger planters, arranging and rearranging the baskets on the patio and in the wheelbarrow and along the walk, bringing the hanging fern and the piggyback plant home directly from the nursery.

There are gardeners with big yards and big dreams . . . and gardeners whose acreage consists of a window box, a clay-potted diffienbachia, and a spray of miniature carnations from the supermarket.

And for all of us, the experience is worthwhile.

The more time I spend with gardens and gardeners, in fact, the more I am convinced that gardens are for gardeners and nongardeners alike. A garden is the source of two separate experiences, two different satisfactions.

There is gardening, and there is being in a garden.

The gardener's experience involves the deep satisfaction of working side by side with the Creator to develop a place of beauty, a safe and life-enhancing environment. The satisfaction of being a gardener is in part the satisfaction of working hard and seeing results. It is also the artist's satisfaction of envisioning something beautiful and rendering that beauty tangible. It is the satisfaction of making the world a better place, of participating in an activity that has been bettering the world for countless centuries.

But the other garden experience is just as valid. It is the experience of just being in a garden, enjoying a garden, gratefully gathering the gifts that the garden has to offer. This is the garden experience anyone can have—even the person who travels and lives in a dark apartment and cannot keep even houseplants alive.

Anyone who wants to can be a gardener.

But anyone, gardener or not, can have a garden in his or her life.

What do I get from being in a garden?

I must confess to being more of the impatient, "I want it now" kind of gardener.

I love to make an excursion to the garden shop and come home with a flat of smiling pansies, all ready to set out in the beds by the door or in a planter on the patio. And I love going out with a basket to pick or cut or pluck the results of what someone else has planted and tended.

Bob is more the farm-in-a-backyard type. He's a different man when he gets out in the garden; he revels in the whole process of feeling the soil on his bare hands, watching over the young sprouts, relocating plants, planning new possibilities. But I enjoy getting out and digging, too, and Bob loves to pick and gather. And we both love having a garden in our lives. Like the lilies and sunflowers and eggplants that surround our home, we both have grown and flourished in our garden.

I suppose I should say "gardens." The property around the converted barn where we live is large enough for us to enjoy a variety of gardening experiences. Along our driveway and over behind the bedrooms, a wooded path winds among fruit trees—orange, avocado, grapefruit, and apricot. A beautiful yellow rosebush climbs around our doorway, but my favorite pink roses, Cecile Brunners, climb in the arbor past the arches to the vegetable garden. Across the driveway, around the pond lies our English garden with its lilies and irises and early blooming bulbs. Winding up the hill is a shady path under spreading birch and pine and sycamore trees that leads up to our big barn-shaped mailbox.

The tree house high in the biggest shamel ash tree has become our "cup of tea" house where my granddaughter Christine likes to host her annual birthday tea party. And then between the garage and the house are the raised gardens where we grow tomatoes, peppers, and eggplant as well as cheerful sunflowers and the fragrant sweet peas that were Bob's Valentine's Day gift to me. Our courtyard garden, which opens off the dining room and our offices, is more my gardening domain. Here a variety of containers hold

> My garden, with its silence and pulses of fragrance that come and go on the airy undulations, affects me like sweet music. Care stops at the gates, and gazes at me wistfully through the bars.
>
> ALEXANDER SMITH

TIME BEGAN IN A GARDEN

(depending on the season) marigolds and strawberries and pink impatiens and my favorite herbs.

What I love best about being surrounded by gardens—aside from the sheer beauty of them—is being able to go out and gather fresh things to enliven my table or beautify my bedroom. I love keeping an old wooden bowl in the kitchen to hold the bounty of the garden: a few onions, some oranges, a green pepper, an eggplant. The soul of a little girl whose garden was a sweet potato in a jar thrills to the idea of going out and gathering her own parsley and cilantro and basil. The other day I even went out and picked a few pansies to decorate a chocolate cake. (They lasted beautifully during the whole dinner party.)

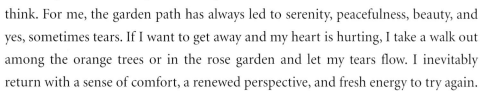

But the garden is so much more to me than a resource for cooking and decorating. To me, the garden is also a refuge, a place to go for rest and spiritual renewal. In the freeway of my life, I love to find an exit ramp that leads to a green retreat. There I can sit still or stroll slowly or dig in the soil and let the serenity of shrub and vine begin to grow inside me.

"I come to the garden alone . . ." begins the old gospel song. And I do that often—in times of pain or difficulty, or when I just need to think. For me, the garden path has always led to serenity, peacefulness, beauty, and yes, sometimes tears. If I want to get away and my heart is hurting, I take a walk out among the orange trees or in the rose garden and let my tears flow. I inevitably return with a sense of comfort, a renewed perspective, and fresh energy to try again.

There have been times in my life when I was in intense pain. And during those hurting times, one of the first things I wanted to do was to go outside and sit on a bench under a tree, to stroll in the dappled light of oak trees or gaze at a fountain. When I did, somehow I would feel safe, comforted, reminded of God's presence. There I could gather strength to go on. There, somehow, my spirit would be renewed . . . re-created.

But I come to the garden in company, too, to share the enjoyment of cool, fragrant breezes and sunny smiles. I love to sit with my Bob out on the patio in the mornings, sharing a cup of coffee or tea and a thought for the day. I love to walk my granddaughter Christine out to the English garden or the rose arbor to gather a bouquet, teaching her what my auntie told me. I love to wander with a friend under the trees and talk about what is happening in our lives. And I'm always game for spreading a blanket on the lawn or in the tree house for an impromptu picnic. Another form of re-creation.

Of course, I've also been re-created while on my knees digging or weeding. There is no law that says you can't experience your garden while you're working in it. In fact, garden work is a perfect setting for re-creation. The combination of fresh air, exercise, and the company of plants is a tonic for the spirit.

But even if you love nothing better than working in the garden, I hope you will also make time to *be* in the garden. I hope you will take the time to be still and experience the paradise you have helped create.

And if you really don't have the time or the space or the inclination to start and maintain a garden, I hope you will find a way to have a flower in your life, even if only by reading about it or by purchasing a bouquet from a street vendor.

At the very least, you can plant a sweet potato in a jar.

You'll like the sight from your kitchen window.

Bringing the Outdoors In

Secrets of a Perfect Bouquet

One of the great joys of growing flowers in the garden is gathering them into bouquets so you can bring the garden inside. Some gardeners even set aside a part of their garden just for bouquets. (Since flowers that do best for cutting are not always the best landscape flowers, many cutting gardens are relegated to hidden corners or even to the vegetable garden.) Cut flowers carefully and "condition" the blooms before arranging them. Here's how:

Getting Them Ready
• Gather flowers when the sun is low—in the morning or evening.
• Use scissors or a sharp knife and cut at a deep angle to provide as much surface as possible for soaking up water. For most flowers, cut when buds are half-open or when some of the buds in a cluster are still closed. Pick zinnias, marigolds, asters, and dahlias in full bloom. Cut stems as long as possible, but try not to take too many unopened buds.
• Get flowers into warm water as quickly as possible; their stems begin to dry after just a few minutes. Some gardeners actually carry a bucket of water and immerse flowers as soon as they are cut.
• Remove the leaves at bottom of stems—those that will be underwater are likely to decay. If flowers were not immediately immersed in water, recut stems and crush bottoms of woody

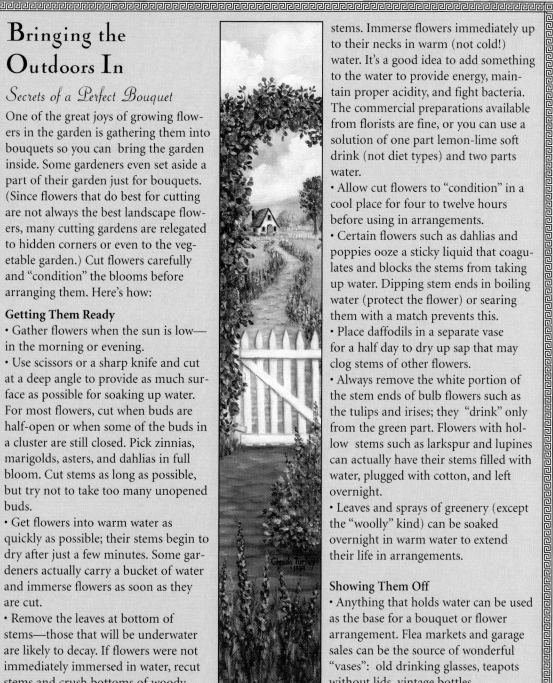

stems. Immerse flowers immediately up to their necks in warm (not cold!) water. It's a good idea to add something to the water to provide energy, maintain proper acidity, and fight bacteria. The commercial preparations available from florists are fine, or you can use a solution of one part lemon-lime soft drink (not diet types) and two parts water.
• Allow cut flowers to "condition" in a cool place for four to twelve hours before using in arrangements.
• Certain flowers such as dahlias and poppies ooze a sticky liquid that coagulates and blocks the stems from taking up water. Dipping stem ends in boiling water (protect the flower) or searing them with a match prevents this.
• Place daffodils in a separate vase for a half day to dry up sap that may clog stems of other flowers.
• Always remove the white portion of the stem ends of bulb flowers such as the tulips and irises; they "drink" only from the green part. Flowers with hollow stems such as larkspur and lupines can actually have their stems filled with water, plugged with cotton, and left overnight.
• Leaves and sprays of greenery (except the "woolly" kind) can be soaked overnight in warm water to extend their life in arrangements.

Showing Them Off
• Anything that holds water can be used as the base for a bouquet or flower arrangement. Flea markets and garage sales can be the source of wonderful "vases": old drinking glasses, teapots without lids, vintage bottles.

Many gourmet soft drinks and waters come in wonderful bottles that can be used as vases. Or you can line baskets, strawberry boxes, and similar containers with plastic and floral foam. Use your imagination.

• Other than containers, you might find the following equipment and materials helpful: "needlepoint" holders to support flowers in place, water-absorbing floral foam, wire netting (to cover the openings of wide-mouthed containers), sharp scissors for cutting stems, reel and stub wire, green floral tape, plus a variety of decorative ribbons and lace.

• Simple arrangements are often the best. Two long-stemmed flowers in a bud vase can be elegant; so can a single blossom floating in a bowl or miniature bouquets in small bottles.

• If your flowers and greens have been properly conditioned, they can be laid directly on the table for an effective centerpiece. Tie them in bunches with ribbon or wind them around candles. They will stay fresh for hours or even days without being in water. You can also place the ends of flowers in water-filled floral tubes tucked out of sight under the greenery.

• Absorbent floral foam is a great arranging tool; it holds stems in place while watering the flowers at the same time. Shape it with a sharp knife, cutting at an angle—don't squeeze it or it will lose its absorbent qualities. Float the foam in water until it sinks by itself and stops bubbling. Then you can tape it into your container with green floral tape and hide both foam and tape with flowers and greens.

• If you have pretty candleholders or a candelabra, discover candle cups, which are little plastic contraptions shaped like funnels and available at florist supply shops. The little round cup on top holds a semicircle of floral foam (like a scoop of ice cream in a cone) and the "funnel" on the bottom fits down into the top of a candle-holder. The "ice cream'" is held in place with tape, a candle is stuck down into the top of the "scoop," and flowers are arranged to cover the ball of foam and the base of the candle. The result is a lovely arrangement with fresh flowers clustered around the base of the candles, above the candle holders.

In Search of a Garden

Do your life circumstances make it difficult for you to create a garden retreat? Any of the following places may offer you a chance to be in a garden. (These are also wonderful sources of gardening ideas.)

A Friend's House: In return for a pitcher of lemonade, a weeding session, or just your friendship, an acquaintance with a lovely yard might allow you some time and space for rest and re-creation.

Public Gardens: If you are lucky enough to live near a botanical garden, visit regularly and enjoy the beauty.

The Zoo: Many zoological parks are beautifully landscaped and provide easy-to-walk pathways and comfortable benches.

The Park: In a medium-sized city, municipal parks or greenways may be your best bet for a touch of green. Look for little parks tucked away downtown or small specialty gardens kept by volunteers.

Historical Sites: The home of a local dignitary or a restored public building may well have restored gardens as well. For a minimal fee (or for free), you can wander through these gardens and dream to your heart's content.

A Local Nursery or Gardening Center: Wonderful for inspiration, instruction, or just to enjoy.

Cemeteries: Older, well-kept graveyards can be peaceful, restorative places.

College Campuses: Many offer landscaped areas designed for study and thought. Some universities also have garden clubs or horticulture classes who maintain lovely gardens.

A Garden Club: Some clubhouses are open to the public and feature the best efforts of many loving hands. Garden clubs also frequently offer tours of local homes.

A People's Garden or Gardening Co-op: Look in your yellow pages, call the newspaper, or ask at a gardening center whether your community has public gardening facilities where you might start a garden or just visit.

These are the things I prize

And hold of dearest worth:

Light of the sapphire skies,

Peace of the silent hills,

Shelter of the forest, comfort of the grass,

Music of birds, murmur of little rills,

Shadows of clouds that swiftly pass,

And, after showers,

The smell of flowers

And of the good brown earth—

And best of all, along the way, friendship and mirth.

HENRY VAN DYKE

Working in the garden gives me something beyond enjoyment of the senses.... It gives me a profound feeling of inner peace. There is no rush toward accomplishment, no blowing of trumpets. Here is the great mystery of life and growth. Everything is changing, growing, aiming at something, but silently, unboastfully, taking its time.

Ruth Stout

A Time for Awakening

A Playground for the Senses

 ake up and smell the roses!

My garden paraphrases that old admonition about coffee and reality into fresh, welcome advice.

"Wake up!" the garden calls to me—a command so gentle it almost feels like coaxing, like Mama shaking me tenderly after a too-long afternoon nap.

Wake up and smell the roses. And while you're sniffing, take in the fragrance of sweet peas and orange blossoms—their delicate or heady fragrances mingling with the rich smell of earth and the tantalizing herbal aromas of basil and thyme.

Standing in my garden, breathing in deep and sweet, I realize how often I seem to be holding my breath. So much of our urban air is noxious, thick. What a relief to find a place where the trees and plants have helped to cleanse the air, where taking a deep breath feels safe and pleasurable. (And what an important reason to keep growing plants, as well as taking steps to nourish the air we breathe!)

But this is not just a matter of breathing cleaner air. It's about finding a place where it's safe to feel. So much about modern living assaults our senses. We're buffeted by bad news, harangued with hurry, assaulted with anxiety, until we unconsciously pull down our awareness levels like blinds on a too-bright window. No wonder we forget to breathe deeply. No wonder we become half-blind, hard-of-hearing, stuffy-nosed, callus-fingered.

No wonder our spirits get hardened to the point that we can discern only the harshest of realities.

But the garden is a safe place to reverse that hardening process, to become conversant with realities that are no less valid for being softer and more beautiful. A garden is a place of tenderness, of freshness, of joy and delight. The triumphs and sorrows here are on the scale of centuries, grounded in the eternal rhythms of the earth.

Here I find myself slowly unfolding, my numbed senses coming alive again. Here it is more than safe. It is wonderful.

My garden is a place that nurtures quiet in the midst of noise and makes it safe to listen to bird song and bee buzz and the trickle of water. People who come here exclaim, "We can't believe we're still in the city."

My garden exudes fragrances that soothe, fragrances that delight, fragrances that linger: a drift of honeysuckle, a waft of orange blossoms, a heady whiff of roses.

We also enjoy pleasing textures of velvet and fuzz and warm and cool and wet and dry. Even the pain—the sting of a bee, the prick of a rose, the itch of a mosquito, the burning of a blister—is easily treated, sometimes by other residents of the garden.

And we eat so well from our garden. Cardboard tomatoes from the supermarket are a planet removed from the luscious globes and ovals we grow in our raised beds. And the tomatoes are just the beginning. Glossy, smooth eggplants; golden, juicy corn; velvety beans—flavored sweetly with my own basil and rosemary—tantalize my tastebuds.

The world will never starve for want of wonders.

G.K.
CHESTERTON

My garden nurtures my sense of wonder as well. The longer I linger, the more there is to see, to smell, to hear and touch and taste and know and wonder about.

I've seen it a million times, and it still amazes me.

I even know a little bit about why and how the garden happens, yet the wonder of it doesn't fade.

I obtain a little seed, perhaps a tiny speck so minuscule I have to mix it with sand or cornmeal to work with it. Fluffing up the soil, I dig a little hole, deposit the seed, and cover it cozily. A little water, a little compost, a little waiting. And before long something green and alive is poking its slender head up out of the soil.

It seems almost trite to call it a miracle, but it is one.

And the miracles happen dependably in my garden, day after day.

Tall lilies wave around my fishpond. If I sit quietly and wait long enough, a long-necked heron will come fishing. And though I chase him away to protect the koi, I marvel at his long-legged grace. If the stilt-legged marauder doesn't pay a visit, I am quieted by the peace of the water, the drifting reflected clouds.

Butterflies love the wildflower meadow behind our rose arbor. And I love the contrast between the exquisite cultivated roses and the exuberant field of poppies and daisies.

As I walk the path to our mailbox in the shade of ash trees and sycamores, I hear the sparrows chattering. If I'm lucky, I may spy a bluebird—an astonishing flash of pure azure. And if I bend down to look among the ground cover, I find that this shaded area conceals wonderful miniature worlds, tiny blossoms, hidden mossy nooks—fairy habitats. (If I take a small child with me, I discover so much more.)

Surprisingly, I find that my sense of humor flourishes in the garden as well. Bob and I laugh together more easily when we're walking in the garden or working together—and the laughter is free, joyful, without sarcasm or cynicism. I don't know why this is, but it must have something to do with perspective, with balance—and because a garden invariably infects me with a sense of playfulness.

Yes, I know there's work to get done. And we get it done, one way or the other. But surely we are missing half the point of gardening if we miss the pleasure and the play that is part of the work.

It's all in the attitude, you see. You can toil and sweat and grit your teeth and subdue the earth.

Or you can toil and sweat and keep your eyes open, your ears alert, your nostrils quivering, your hands ready to reach out and touch. You can work with senses alert for the experience. You can *be* instead of just *do*. And then your work will take on a spirit of gratitude, of joy—yes, of playfulness.

Come play, the garden beckons me, even when I'm mopping my brow. And if I let it, the child in me is running outside, slamming the door behind me, ready to soak up the wonder of it all.

So come with me and play in my garden. Wake up and smell the roses—and then listen and look and touch and taste.

Open your eyes to the kaleidoscope of colors that is peculiar to your part of the country and to your very own garden: the long parade of growing in the South, the ever-changing drama of the northern seasons, the special plants and conditions of your particular region. Enjoy the wild abandon of the cottage garden, the geometric serenity of a formal garden, the shaded coolness of a woodland garden.

Reach out and touch the trees and flowers and soil. Let the cool water trickle over your toes, the rich dirt run through your fingers, your backside grow cold from sitting on stone benches or the ground.

The Fragrant Garden
Plants That Make
Good Scents

All the following flowers, herbs, and shrubs contribute to the lovely fragrance of a garden. Double flowers often put off a stronger scent. But be careful: Not every variety of every flower listed will be fragrant. For example, some daffodils have almost no scent. Also, check with your local nursery to make sure your selections will grow well in your region.

alyssum • artemisia
butterfly bush • candytuft
chamomile • crocus • daffodil
daylily • flowering tobacco
four o'clock • freesia
gardenia • geranium, scented
heliotrope • honeysuckle
hyacinth • iris • jasmine
lavender • lemon balm
lemon thyme • lemon verbena
lilac • mignonette • mint
moonflower • narcissus
petunia • pinks • primrose
rose • sage
snowdrop • sweet pea
sweet woodruff
violet

Setting the Stage for a Symphony

Attracting Birds to Your Garden

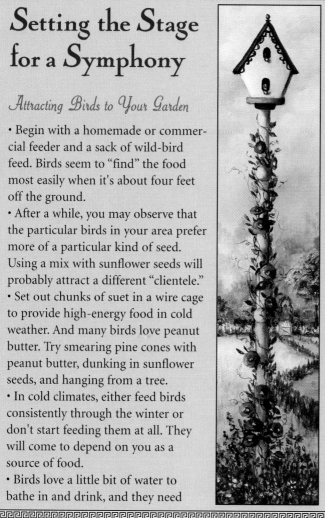

• Begin with a homemade or commercial feeder and a sack of wild-bird feed. Birds seem to "find" the food most easily when it's about four feet off the ground.

• After a while, you may observe that the particular birds in your area prefer more of a particular kind of seed. Using a mix with sunflower seeds will probably attract a different "clientele."

• Set out chunks of suet in a wire cage to provide high-energy food in cold weather. And many birds love peanut butter. Try smearing pine cones with peanut butter, dunking in sunflower seeds, and hanging from a tree.

• In cold climates, either feed birds consistently through the winter or don't start feeding them at all. They will come to depend on you as a source of food.

• Birds love a little bit of water to bathe in and drink, and they need places near the feeding area in which to perch or hide from predators. (If you're lucky, they will nest there as well.) If your garden doesn't have trees and shrubs for this purpose, plant some!

• Attract hummingbirds by planting the kinds of flowers they prefer. Many of them are partial to red and orange flowers, and they like long, tubular flowers such as salvias and trumpet vines. Hummingbirds also like a moving water source, such as a fountain or waterfall. Avoid herbicides and pesticides.

• If you use a commercial hummingbird feeder, follow the manufacturer's instructions for mixing the sugar-water solution. Never use sugar substitutes or honey. Be alert for mold in the solution; it can kill the birds. Periodically wash the feeder, rinse thoroughly, and sterilize with hot water.

• Hang bird feeders and hummingbird plants close to your window so you can enjoy the show. If you hang a lace curtain in the window, you can watch the birds at close range without disturbing them.

Wake up to a symphony of bird song, a rooster's crow, the laughter of children, even a string quartet playing a concert alfresco.

Here, the senses can rejoice. Here a sense of wonder is awakened. Here life comes back into balance, closer to the way things were meant to be.

I know I'm alive.

And I'm having a wonderful time.

To Everything There Is a Seasoning

An Herbal Primer

Almost since the beginning of time, herbs have been prized residents of the garden. They have been used as medicines, as preservatives, as household products. Today, however, they are valued primarily for their flavor and their scent—they brighten up our meals and freshen the air both indoors and in the garden itself. Herbs are generally hardy and easy to grow either outdoors or in containers; many actually prefer poor soil and dry conditions. I like to grow basil and rosemary together in pots surrounded by marigolds for color.

15 Herbs to Grow for Fragrance and Flavor

• **BASIL:** This member of the mint family has a spicy, appetizing flavor and aroma. It complements tomatoes beautifully and is an essential ingredient in pesto. Use it with pasta, fish, chicken, or in salads.

• **BAY:** Bay leaves, which grow on an aromatic shrub, are used in almost every kind of cooking and are indispensable for soups and stews. Their graceful oval shape also makes them useful as a garnish.

• **CHERVIL:** Introduced to northern Europe by the Romans, this is a classic herb in French cooking. Its leaves, which smell faintly of aniseed, lose their flavor quickly and should be added to a dish just before serving. Good with egg or cheese dishes or as a garnish for creamy soups. Often used to flavor vinegar.

• **CORIANDER (CILANTRO):** This herb is characteristic of Indian, Chinese, and Mexican cuisines. Both the leaves and the seeds of this spicy plant are used in curries. Also good in salads.

• **CHIVES:** This mild member of the onion family adds a delicate onion-like flavor and aroma to salads, egg and cheese dishes, and dips. The round pink flowers make an attractive garnish.

• **DILL:** The feathery leaves of this distinctly flavored herb are used in salads, fish dishes, and sauces. The seeds are used to make sauerkraut and dill pickles.

• **LAVENDER:** Although lavender may be used to flavor syrups and cream for desserts, it is used more often for its sweet, pungent smell. For centuries lavender has been used to scent linens, spice potpourri, and also to ward off insects.

• **MARJORAM/OREGANO:** These are different herbs with a similar spicy taste; they pair well together or with parsley and also team up beautifully with garlic to spice up tomatoes, eggplant and zucchini, beef and cheese. They are often used in Italian, Greek, Mexican, and Provençal cuisines.

• **MINT:** This refreshing herb grows in multiple varieties; there is even a chocolate mint. A traditional accompaniment to lamb, it is also widely used to flavor fruits, sweets, and drinks. All varieties are effective flea and tick repellents. Unlike many herbs, mint likes to grow where there is a lot of water. It propagates widely and will take over an herb bed, so it's best to keep it in a confined space.

• **PARSLEY:** Available both in the familiar curly-leaved and the flat-leaved Italian variety, parsley is widely used both as a garnish and as a flavoring element for meat, poultry, fish, and vegetables. Try it to add a festive color and a cool flavor to soups. Mincing a dried herb such as oregano with a sprig of parsley will freshen the taste of the dried herb. I like to keep my parsley in a vase of water as I would a posy. It will keep a week or two in the refrigerator.

• **ROSEMARY:** The leaves of this evergreen have a distinct piny smell. Rosemary goes well with lamb, fish, and rice dishes. It is best used fresh because the dried leaves lose flavor and become spiky.

• **SAGE:** Bob Cratchit's children exclaimed over the delicious aroma of sage with their Christmas goose. The silvery leaves of this herb are especially useful for seasoning fatty meats and sausages.

• **SUMMER SAVORY:** The strong, slightly bitter flavor is reminiscent of thyme and pairs especially well with peas and beans. The winter variety has a stronger flavor and is considered inferior.

• **TARRAGON:** This strongly flavored herb is used to season delicate sauces and egg and cheese dishes. It is also popularly used to flavor vinegar for salads and sauces.

• **THYME** A versatile and fragrant herb, thyme teams well with parsley in a variety of dishes from chicken and pork to zucchini and tomatoes. In addition to common garden thyme, there are varieties with lemon, caraway, or other flavors.

Cooking with Herbs

Using herbs effectively in cooking is largely a matter of practice, but here are some basic recipes. See chapter 3 for information on how to dry and freeze herbs.

BOUQUET GARNI

This little bundle of herbs is a classic ingredient in French cooking. Use to flavor soups and stews. Use fresh herbs, if possible, but you can also use chopped, dried herbs tied up in little squares of cheesecloth. Store in tightly covered container.

> 4 sprigs parsley
> 2 sprigs thyme
> 1 bay leaf
> 1 sprig chervil
> 1 sprig marjoram

Tie stems of herbs together with string. Use one bundle for every two quarts of soup, and add about 20 minutes before the soup is done. Before serving, pull out bouquet garni and discard.

FINES HERBES

This blend of herbs adds delightful flavor to cheese and egg dishes. Again, fresh is best, but you can use dried herbs tied in a cheesecloth bundle.

> 1 sprig each parsley, tarragon, chervil, and chives

Mince finely and add to dish just before serving.

> A garden is
>
> a place to feel
>
> the beauty
>
> of solitude.
>
> BOB BARNES

HERBAL SALT SUBSTITUTE

> 1 tablespoon each ground dried basil, coriander, thyme
> 2 teaspoons each ground cumin, onion powder, ground dried parsley
> 1 teaspoon each garlic powder, ground mustard, sweet Hungarian paprika, cayenne, and kelp

Grind all herbs with mortar and pestle. Mix ingredients and place on table as a salt replacement. Vary herbs and spices to suit your taste.

TARRAGON VINEGAR

Try other herbs as well (garlic, chive, dill, marjoram, sage, cilantro)—and any kind of vinegar you like (experiment with different flavors). Use in salads and sauces. Use the same basic technique to make herbed olive oil.

> ⅔ cup tarragon, lightly packed
> 1 cup vinegar

Pick herbs before they flower, and bruise them with the flat of a knife. Place in clear, sterile quart jars and add vinegar. Cover with nonmetal lids and steep for two weeks in a warm, dark place. Shake occasionally. When herbs have steeped, strain vinegar through cheesecloth and discard herbs. Add sprigs of fresh herbs to sterilized bottles and add vinegar. Cork and store in a cool place.

HOMEMADE HERBAL TEA

Herbal teas are calorie- and caffeine-free and can be soothing. But herb teas are not totally benign. Many have medicinal effects and should not be drunk in large quantities. Chamomile tea may trigger allergic reactions in people who are sensitive to ragweed.

Use 1 teaspoon dried herbs (mint, chamomile, thyme, or a mixture) per cup of water. Place herbs in warmed teapot, pour water over herbs, cover, and let steep 3 to 5 minutes.

Gently steed our spirits,

carrying with them dreams of flowers.

William Wordsworth

A Time for Dreaming

The Joy of Endless Possibilities

n your dreams, how does your garden grow?

Is it a window box full of petunias and pinks like the ones you saw in Germany?

Is it a wandering path through blooming bushes, a series of surprises like you remember from your great-aunt's house?

Does your dream feature wisteria dripping from a trellis or roses climbing a garden gate or water lilies sunning themselves in a pond?

Or do you dream about pots of greenery in the corners of your rooms and graceful bouquets gracing your tabletops?

All this is important to consider because your dreams are where your garden begins.

Long before the first piece of sod is turned, long before the seeds are ordered or the plants are purchased or the first buds begin to open, the garden takes root in the mind, the heart, the imagination. And even after a garden has begun, it continues to be fed from the gardener's dreams.

In the North, where snow tucks in the earth for its long winter nap, it's easy to spot the garden dreamers. They're the ones inside on snowy afternoons with a cup of tea and the big stack of seed catalogs—those bright, glossy "wish books" with their pages and pages of glorious blooms. But even we southern Californians, who garden for three seasons and manage to have some kind of green lawn year-round, still feed our dreams on the catalogs. Bob and I take them on vacation with us, and we browse through them in our idle moments. Who can resist all those marvelous possibilities?

Dreaming, in fact, is one of gardening's great joys—equal almost to the joy of seeing one's dreams gradually unfurl into green reality. And each successive dream-come-true gives way to yet another possibility.

We gardeners are always in the process of picturing the next phase of our perennial borders or the newest choice for our cutting gardens or next year's plans for our vegetable plots. We are continually assessing what has gone right and what has gone wrong and what might work better and what would be simply wonderful.

"Perhaps another row of larkspur there—and I need a taller varietal."

"I think we could put in an arbor with climbing roses and morning glories—and I want some zinnias for the house."

"That color of cosmos is definitely too much over by the porch, but wouldn't it be great out next to the fence?"

And by the time the bulb catalogs arrive, we are hungry to begin dreaming of even more possibilities.

Garden dreams are ever-renewing, a source of ongoing energy and passion. They are the impetus to our plans, the motivation that keeps us fighting the bugs and the weeds and the callouses. It is our dreams that get us started and our dreams that keep us going, our dreaming minds nurtured by the very beauty and stillness and serenity our earlier dreams have inspired and our hard work has made possible.

Even in my garden-deprived young life, I encountered places and plants that planted in me a dream, a seed of "someday." I remember drives through the country when my dad would stop the car and let us play in the cotton fields. And excursions with my brother to the creek behind our rented house to gather watercress for my dad's gourmet salads and sandwiches. And trips to the florist with my mother to spend rare extra cash on something beautiful. ("Fresh is best," she always insisted.)

And I'll never forget my first garden party years later, after Bob and I had moved to the lovely seaside town of Newport Beach. A woman in our church invited me to tea, and we sat on a brick patio overlooking a stretch of bright-blue sea dotted with sailboats. All around us were great urns abloom with daisies, hanging baskets trailing ivy, clusters of containers bright with impatiens.

Yes, I told myself deep in my heart. Yes. That is what I want in my life. Slowly the dreams took shape . . . and gradually, over the years, have come to fruition.

I've talked to so many friends whose memories shaped their garden dreams and, eventually, their gardens.

One friend remembers family workdays in the yard. She and her parents and brothers and sisters would spend the morning mowing and raking and weeding, then gather on the patio for a barbecue while the smell of wet leaves and cut grass still hung in the air.

Another friend remembers a green-thumbed grandmother who tucked a garden in every corner of her tiny property, raising fluffy-headed peonies and elegant irises and dainty violets set out in a circle around her biggest trees. She would fuss at children who carelessly ran into her yard, but she also gave away her flowers freely to passing little ones, carefully encasing their stems in wet tissue so they would survive the trip home.

Some people remember visits to Europe and strolls in magnificently blooming public gardens—or happy hours spent in parks and botanical gardens wherever they were raised. Some recall summer evenings when the fragrance of a neighbor's flowering shrubs drifted over the fences.

How many gardens, I wonder, have been conceived and planted on the basis of remembered sights and sounds and smells from childhood? How many rosebushes have been chosen and ordered and planted and carefully tended, because the gardener remembered that particular rose from the old homestead with its tiny pink bloom and peppery smell? How many vegetable plots have been established on a memory of vine-ripened tomatoes and summer-fresh beans on Grandma's table?

And how many men and women of the past, in planting their gardens, also unwittingly planted a gardener?

But garden dreams are more complex than mere memories. What we are really talking about is why people create gardens in the first place—and why we keep on digging and trimming and digging. Our garden dreams are our motivations, our energy sources, our sources of love. And garden dreams are as various and diverse as the gardens themselves.

Some people who garden simply want a flower on the table, an herb in the stew, a tomato in the salad.

Some enjoy being garden scientists: testing the soil, experimenting with seeds and grafts, carefully recording the results.

There are homemakers, driven by their nesting instincts to surround their living space with beauty, and artists striving to paint an ever-changing picture with living, three-dimensional forms.

Some people garden for the challenge of raising the perfect rose, of placing the perfect row of graceful daylilies in front of the perfect stand of vigilant hollyhocks.

Some respond to the call of ever-renewing life, because they are invigorated and renewed by being involved with such an astounding miracle as growth.

And some people garden simply because they love being in a garden, and gardening is the best way they know to get there.

However your dream garden grows, it lives in anticipation. It also requires silence and careful listening to the demands of your heart as well as to the realities of your climate and landscape. Sometimes you even need to pull back from your everyday realities in order to dream effectively. You need to withdraw from the demands of now in order to think about tomorrow's possibilities.

Maybe that's why the dormant wintertime is such a fruitful season for northern gardeners. And maybe that's why Bob and I do such effective dreaming while we're on vacation. But we also like to wander around our garden sometimes

when our minds and hands are "off duty," without shears or hoe or basket, simply enjoying. In those quiet times, when we talk or just be, our most wonderful dreams are born—not only for our gardens but for our entire lives.

Most garden dreams thrive on hope—for what is a dream but imaginative hoping? And gardeners, as a group, are the most hopeful people I know.

It takes a measure of hope to make even the simplest beginning—to buy a little pot, a bag of soil. It takes a hopeful spirit to see anemones and chrysanthemums in a strip of undecorated sod or bare dirt, to envision daffodils when the eye sees only snow—even to expect that a scrawny little bunch of leaves in a new pot will choose to grow and flower.

It takes hope, in other words, to start a garden.

But the garden itself is what really teaches you how to hope.

The hope in a gardener's heart is strengthened every year by the experience of watching green settle in a filmy veil over bare branches, watching a bare, raked plot of ground suddenly explode with busy, purposeful growth.

Hope is nurtured every time a pruned-back bush sends forth invigorated shoots, every time a languishing bush flourishes in a new location, every time a self-seeded volunteer crops up in a new location as a lovely surprise. Hope is nurtured just by being in the company of trees and plants and flowers, by witnessing the relentless strength and energy of growing things.

Not that there aren't disappointments . . . and the occasional heartbreak.

That expensive peony you've nurtured so carefully may never hold up its heavy head. Aphids and snails may defy your most diligent efforts. The neighbor's dog may dig up two feet of your prized perennial border. A whole year's peaches may turn out green and hard and sour.

But there's always next year.

You have another chance.

In fact, that's the most hopeful lesson I've learned in more than thirty years of gardening. Plants as a whole are far hardier and more forgiving than most people ever imagine. There are almost no fatal mistakes and very few serious ones. You always have the chance to start over.

My friend Anne teaches an art class to a group of second graders. The first

rule they must learn in the class is that no one is allowed to say, "I messed up." That doesn't mean that mistakes aren't allowed! But she wants them to learn that mistakes aren't fatal. So instead of saying, "I messed up," they learn to say, "I want to try again." Instead of dwelling on their failures, they are encouraged to say, "I'd like a new piece of paper."

That's exactly the way the garden works. You always have a fresh piece of paper. You can always try again.

And best of all, you can always keep dreaming.

Everlasting Dreams
Secrets of Preserving Your Blossoms

It's always a bit sad to see the beautiful blooms in your garden wilt and die. But with a little effort, the scents and colors of flowers and herbs can be preserved for years to come.

Methods of Preservation

• **AIR DRYING:** This is by far the simplest and most practical way to preserve flowers, but you need a warm, dark, well-ventilated place—an attic, closet, or furnace room—where the drying flowers and herbs can hang undisturbed for weeks at a time. Pick flowers in the morning after the dew has dried but before the sun has grown hot—and do this before they begin to drop their petals. Then simply hang the plants upside down in a warm place to dry. Hang large flowers individually, small flowers and herbs in bunches bound by rubber bands. (String tends to slip as the stems shrink.) This method works well for most flowers. Very thick flowers (such as roses), which tend to get damp and mold, and very fragrant flowers, which tend to turn brown, are best dried with a quicker process. Individual petals for potpourri can be air-dried on frames or dried in the microwave.

• **DESSICANT DRYING:** A dessicant is simply a material that absorbs moisture and thereby hastens the drying process. Cornmeal, borax, and sand are all useful dessicants, or you can buy at craft stores a material called silica gel, which changes color to show it has absorbed moisture. The basic process of drying with a dessicant is to pour the material carefully around the flower in a wood or cardboard box, making sure it supports the head and gets between the petals. When the flowers are thoroughly dry (after about a week or two), they should be lifted carefully out of the dessicant and the particles should be brushed away with a small, dry brush. Dessicant drying is usually not appropriate for herbs that will be used as food.

• MICROWAVE DRYING: This very quick method is good for small quantities of petals or herbs or for flowers high in moisture or fragrant oils that might darken if air-dried. Color retention is good with this method, but the microwave tends to make the flowers collapse, so it's a good idea to put flowers in a bed of silica gel for support. To dry a large flower in a box of silica gel, microwave on low for two minutes, let stand ten minutes, then check to see how the flower looks before microwaving some more. To dry herbs or petals for potpourri, place between sheets of paper towels and microwave on medium several minutes. Replace towels as needed and repeat until petals or herbs are crisp. Because microwaves vary in power, you may have to experiment to find the optimal setting and time.

• PRESSING: This method preserves flowers and leaves in a flat state suitable for use on pictures, note cards, invitations, and so forth. Plants should be harvested when perfectly dry and placed carefully in position, then pressed between two absorbent sheets covered by some kind of weight. For centuries flowers have been pressed in books, but this method often resulted in stained books. A better method is to press

the plants between pages of a large municipal phonebook—or simply lay a weight on a stack of newspapers with the plants tucked inside and leave undisturbed for several weeks to two months, until the flowers are absolutely dry and flat. Then they can be secured with white glue or rubber cement onto whatever background is desired. Use tweezers to handle the delicate blossoms.

• FREEZING: Freezing is an excellent way to preserve the fresh flavor of certain herbs, especially basil, chervil, chives, dill, marjoram, oregano, parsley, sage, and thyme. Tie up small bunches of herbs and blanch one minute in boiling water. Plunge in ice water for two minutes, pat dry, and quick-freeze in plastic freezer bags. You can simply chop chives and parsley and put directly into plastic bags. And mint, lemon balm, and borage flowers can be added to ice-cube trays, covered with water, and frozen for adding to drinks.

Everlasting Projects

• HERB AND FLOWER WREATHS: Use an assortment of plants—mint, parsley, artemisia, basil, sage, or whatever catches your fancy. Dry in little bundles of five to seven stems. When dry, use florist's pins or glue to attach the bundles to a straw wreath. (If you use pins, leave the plastic wrapping on the wreath; it will "catch" the pins better.

Alternate colors and textures, and overlap leaves to cover stems, working from inner to outer edge. Accent finished wreath with dried flowers or a bow. Hang it up so you can see where you need to trim or fill in.

A very simple wreath can be made with long cuts of silvery artemisia. Simply lay the fresh artemisia in a wreath shape around the inside of a round plastic mesh laundry basket. Keep in a warm, dark place until artemisia is completely dry, then remove carefully from the basket. The artemisia will have taken on the round shape of the basket. Bind the wreath lightly with dental floss to hold it together, then decorate as desired. This method can also be used with ivy, eucalyptus, or any kind of leafy vine.

Another idea is to use a glue gun to attach dried flowers and other materials to three-inch wooden curtain rings. Add little bows and use to decorate packages, hang in small nooks, or give as gifts.

• POTPOURRI: For many centuries, stately homes and mansions have scented their rooms with fragrant mixtures of dried flowers and herbs, fragrant woods and bark, and essential oils. Now you can find bags of potpourri in gift and hobby stores, but it's fun to make your own.

Essentially, there are two kinds of potpourri: dry and moist. I prefer to make the dry kind by mixing rose and other flower petals, dried slices of orange and lemon, spices, essential oils, and a fixative that helps preserve the scent. The potpourri oils you find in craft stores are usually synthetic and premixed. They are inexpensive and smell fine, but they don't last long and rarely come in pure, single-flower fragrances. We prefer to use essential oils, which are natural oils extracted from single sources. We order ours through the mail, but you will probably have your best luck at a big health-food store. Ask there, too, about orris root powder (to use as a fixative). This powder comes from the root of an iris and has a faint violet smell. If you can't find the orris root powder, you can do without the fixative or substitute vermiculite, a substance found in many garden stores.

Here is a basic potpourri recipe you can adapt to what you have on hand:

BASIC GARDEN POTPOURRI

> 3 cups main flower petals (roses, lavenders, or a mixture of petals)
> ½ to 1 cup complementary herbs and leaves (try thyme, rosemary, lemon verbena)
> 6 tablespoons spices, crushed (cinnamon, cloves)
> ½ cup dried citrus slices (slice thin and place on a cookie sheet, dry in oven overnight at 200 degrees)
> 1 ½ ounces orris root powder or vermiculite
> 6 drops or less scented oils (rose, lavender, orange blossom)

Combine dried flowers and leaves in a large glass or ceramic mixing bowl. Crush spices with mortar and pestle; if you are using orris root, crush it, too. Add these to flowers and herbs and mix with fingers. If you are using vermiculite as a fixative, mix with oil in a covered jar; add oil to vermiculite until mixture is scented but not oily. Carefully blend vermiculite mixture with petals and spices until mixture is fragrant. If you are working with very delicate petals, you may want to work them in after you've added the oil. If you used orris root, mix it first with the petals, then add oil to the mixture a drop at a time until the scent seems strong enough. Place the mixture in a large Ziploc bag, seal tightly, and store in a dark place about six weeks until the fragrance mellows. Shake the bag every other day to mix. Once your potpourri has mellowed, place in a pretty open bowl and enjoy.

As you mix your potpourri, strive for a pleasing mix of colors, fragrances, and textures. You can add bark, pine cones, sycamore balls, or other elements for texture—and vary the oils as well.

After a number of months, the scent of the potpourri will begin to fade. You can renew it by putting it back in the Ziploc bag, adding a few drops of the same oil, and leaving it sealed for 24 hours.

• SCENTS FOR BED AND BATH: The same basic ingredients you use for potpourri can become the base for fragranced items throughout your home. For instance, your potpourri mixture, ground in a coffee grinder or blender and stuffed into little muslin or calico bags, can serve as sachets in drawers and closets. For an extra-pretty sachet, make little lace hearts lined with tulle or netting and fill with potpourri, or wrap a little potpourri in a lace handkerchief and tie with a narrow ribbon. If you used a mixture of vermiculite and essential oils for your potpourri, that mixture can be used to fill sachets as well.

Here are some other ideas for using your preserved garden to sweeten your bed and bath:

MOTH-REPELLING SACHET

> 2 tablespoons each cedar chips, lavender flowers, rosemary leaves, and wormwood leaves (or choose from bay leaves, patchouli, costmary, peppermint, rosemary, rue, southernwood, or sassafras, which repel moths as well)
> ½ teaspoon cedar essential oil
> ⅛ teaspoon camphor essential oil, nonsynthetic (optional)
> 6-inch square of thin, tightly woven muslin or calico
> 8 inches ribbon or string

Combine herbs and oil and grind or blend. Cut the fabric with pinking shears. Place a heaping tablespoon of sachet powder in the center, bring corners together, and tie with ribbon or string. Tuck bags in closets and drawers to repel moths. Lightly crush to release more scent. Recharge with essential oils every year or two.

DREAM PILLOWS

The dream pillow is an old and charming way to encourage sweet sleep and sweet dreams. The ingredients can vary; each herb carries a different significance. I don't know if I believe in the specific connotations here, but the aroma is certainly dreamy.

> ½ cup hops (to encourage sleep)
> ⅛ cup lavender flowers (to make dreams pleasant)
> ⅛ cup rosemary leaves (to help sleeper recall dreams)
> ⅛ cup thyme (to prevent nightmares)
> 2 tablespoons mugwort leaves (to instill dreams)
> ⅛ cup rose petals (for dreams of love)

Blend ingredients and sew into small muslin pillows. Tuck inside pillowcase at night. Or sew a pretty pillow with a little pocket on the outside to hold the dream pillow. Give as a gift with a card to explain. This would make a nice gift for a spouse.

ROSES UPON ROSES BATH SACHET

> ½ cup quick oats
> ½ cup dried rose petals
> ¼ cup dried rose geranium leaves
> ½ cup table salt
> 2 teaspoons rose oil
> 6 small muslin bags in shades of pink and rose

Mix oatmeal and herbs in a bowl. Put mixture into bags and tie with twine or waterproof ribbon, making a bow or loop. After you have filled the tub, swish sachet through hot water a few times, or hang it under the running water as the tub fills. Hang sachet on the faucet to dry; it can be used several times. For guests, place bags in a basket in your bathroom with a little note about how to use. Try different combinations of herbs and oils such as rosemary with lavender oil or pine oil.

PEPPERMINT FOOT BATH

Boil 8 cups water. Add 1 tablespoon table salt and five sprigs of fresh or ten sprigs of dried peppermint (or use another kind of mint, rosemary, or lemon verbena). Let stand until water is warm and comfortable. Pour into bowl and soak your feet 10 to 20 minutes. Rinse with cold water and apply lotion.

More than half a century has passed, and yet each spring, when I wander into the primrose wood and see the pale yellow blooms, and smell their sweetest of scents . . . for a moment I am seven years old again and wandering in the fragrant wood.

GERTRUDE JEKYLL

How Will Your Garden Grow?

Are you dreaming of something different in your garden—or just wondering where to start? There are many different ways your garden can grow.

• ANNUAL BED—fresh every year. Simply prepare the soil and plant when the last frost is over, or start seeds indoors and transplant when the weather warms.

• BUTTERFLY GARDEN—designed to attract butterflies. Good plants for a butter-fly garden include bergamot, butterfly weed, daylily, delphinium, lupine, milkweed, nas-turtium, red salvia, and violets. Butterflies also need protection from the wind, a place to lay eggs and build cocoons, and a source of water.

• CONTAINER GARDEN—lets you garden even if you don't have a garden, and gives you extra space if you do. Almost any con-tainer—from an empty can to an old wheel-barrow to a child's red wagon—can hold your garden. Just punch holes or place a layer of rocks on the bottom for drainage.

• CUTTING GARDEN—set aside a small plot to grow flowers specially for bouquets and arrangements. These gardens tend to be less attractive out-of-doors so some gardeners hide them in out-of-the-way places or even grow them in their vegetable gardens.

• KITCHEN GARDEN—a small plot near your back door that provides some basic vegetables (leaf lettuce, tomatoes, beans), favorite herbs, and a few flowers. The idea is a manageable plot that is readily at hand for kitchen duty.

• A LITERARY GARDEN—enjoy the rich associa-tions between gardens and literature. A popular form is a Shakespeare garden planted with flowers and herbs mentioned by the Bard. But you could also do a Bible garden, a Thomas Wolfe garden, or a Beatrix Potter garden. Or take a hint from Olive Ann Burns: "Over yonder were what she called her 'word plants'—the wildflowers she planted because they had names she liked. Creepin Charlie, Lizzie run by the fence, love's a-bustin', fetch me some ivy cause Baby's got the croup."

• MESCLUN GARDEN—a salad mix of lettuces and herbs grown and harvested together when very young. Mesclun mixes are available through commercial nurseries and mail-order houses, or you can put together your own mix of greens.

• MOONLIGHT GARDEN—a collection of white flowers planted together to achieve a wonderful glowing effect in the moonlight. Because many white flowers are also very fragrant, the effect can be enchanting.

• PERENNIAL BORDER—combines vari-ous long-lived flowers and shrubs in a har-monious mixture of sizes, textures, and colors along the edge of a lawn, path, building, or fence. The plants used are perennials, meaning they do not have to be replanted every year.

• SCENTED GARDEN—planted primarily for aroma in the garden itself, in cut-flower arrangements, and for potpourri and dried flowers. See chapter 2 for a list of possible flowers to plant.

• WILDFLOWER MEADOW—enjoy poppies in California, bluebonnets in Texas, trillium and wild roses in New Jersey, and Queen Anne's lace everywhere. But don't break the law and dig flowers up from the wild—seeds are widely available.

If seeds in the black earth can turn into such beautiful

roses, what might not the heart of man become in its long

journey toward the stars?

G. K. Chesterton

A Time for Growing

Daily Lessons and Tender Miracles

I hadn't been involved with plants for more than a season before I began to realize what was happening.

I had thought I was growing my garden, when actually my garden was growing me. Teaching me. Making me wiser.

I used to garden almost entirely for the results. I liked having flowers on my windowsill, so I knew I had to dig in the soil and plant the seeds and pull the weeds and drag around the watering hose. I loved picking fresh herbs and vegetables for my table, so I knew I had to fertilize and mulch and prune and pick. (Sometimes, in certain seasons, I have to pick and pick and pick!)

But the longer I'm involved with the garden, the more I'm learning to appreciate the process of gardening. And I'm coming to appreciate more and more the lessons my garden can teach me if I only pay attention.

Of course, I'm not the first person to discover that the garden is really an institute of higher learning, the plants and flowers beautiful visual aids.

I think of the ancient Egyptians learning the lessons of watering and fertilizing around the Nile, of the wandering Hebrews learning the lay of the Promised Land, of Plato and Socrates and their students learning philosophy in the groves around Athens.

I think of Jesus advising the crowds to "consider the lilies of the field . . ." and learn from them.

I think of Aristotle's student Theophrastus, the father of botany, writing down the observations that influenced gardeners and scientists through the centuries . . . of the ninth-century monk Walafrid Strabo patiently recording his herbal discoveries in the monastery of St. Gallen . . . of the winter-weary Pilgrims learning from their Native American hosts to fertilize corn with pieces of fish . . . of intrepid nineteenth-century plant collectors sailing around the world to collect new and unheard of specimens.

And I think of Bob and me, starting with pots of geraniums in our tiny apartment, planting trees and flower beds in our "starter" home, growing ferns and impatiens in our townhouse, putting in raised beds around the remodeled barn where we now live.

So much to learn. So much growing to do.

And for the most part, what a gentle, forgiving teacher. My garden teaches by the soundest of methods. It lets me try new things and then learn from my successes and failures.

What does my garden teach? On the most prosaic level, my garden teaches me about gardening—often lessons no book or nursery or helpful neighbor or agricultural service can impart. It even promotes book learning, when events I've observed in my garden send me to the shelves to find out why.

And my particular garden teaches me about itself, if I have the sense to pay attention. It has its own unique ecology, this little patch of land where we hoe and plant and pick. It has its unique soil and climatic conditions, its unique slope and

TIME BEGAN IN A GARDEN

rocks and pollution levels. Knowing what works here and what doesn't has taken time and attention and a fair amount of experimentation.

When we lived in Newport Beach, for example, we had no trouble growing beautiful ferns and impatiens. Then we moved to Riverside, with its semiarid climate and hot summers, and all those beautiful water-loving plants shriveled up. In addition, oil from a long-forgotten tank had leached out into the soil in part of our garden, poisoning it for healthy growth. It took us years to learn what shade and water and compost and truckloads of topsoil would allow us to grow and what just wasn't worth the effort.

Our garden taught us another lesson about fertilizer. When we first began keeping chickens, we knew that their manure was good for the plants, so we put it directly on the soil. It only took us one season to learn that straight chicken manure was too "hot"; it burned the tender roots and limited our yield. We learned to put the chicken manure into the compost heap and let it sit awhile, and now we have wonderful results with our home-grown fertilizer.

You can learn a lot about gardening in books. You can even watch videos and TV shows. But gardening is also the ultimate hands-on learning experience. Hands on, Bob and I have learned an astonishing amount about our home and the land that surrounds it.

We've learned other things as well. We're not the first gardeners to discover that garden lessons reach far beyond the confines of the garden walls. In the laboratory of our garden, I have learned many beautiful, sometimes painful, lessons about how the world is ordered, about how I can live my life better.

Bob says that people who do a good job of managing their lives probably do a good job of managing their gardens, too. But the reverse is also true, I've found. Learning to manage a garden teaches you a lot about managing your life.

One lesson I'm trying to remember has to do with who I am in the scheme of things.

I'm here as a helper, a facilitator, a guide.

I'm removing obstacles that keep my plants from growing or guiding their growth in a desirable direction or helping them concentrate their energy on the business of growing. I'm deciding which plants have a right to grow in a particular space.

But I'm not really growing anything.

They're growing themselves. And I'm allowed to be in on the process.

I have to remember always that plants (and people) *want* to grow. Seeds want to sprout. Flowers want to bud, to bloom. Trees want to produce fruit. Children want to become adults.

Life is so strong, so viable, so persistent. Plants will overcome all manner of obstacles to survive. Remembering that gives me the confidence to try something new (or something old I had forgotten), to make mistakes, to experiment.

I've heard it said that the most difficult task in life is learning what we can control and what we can't control—then acting appropriately. That's the whole point behind the famous Serenity Prayer: "Lord, give me the serenity to accept the things I can't change, the courage to change the things I can, and the wisdom to know the difference." Most of us need help walking the fine line between helplessness and overcontrol.

My garden helps me learn to walk that fine line more gracefully.

If I want to have a garden, I must take the responsibility to prepare the soil, to plant the seeds or the seedlings or the bulbs, to mulch and weed and water and feed. I must watch out for disease and for harmful insects and for extremes of weather. If I neglect any of those responsibilities, my garden will pay the price.

And yet I can do all those things and still have a bad year in the garden. A hailstorm or a flood or an infestation of hornworms can wipe out an entire crop or a whole section of my perennial border. The neighbor's dog (or my own dog) can go digging in my freshly planted cutting garden. Or rabbits can eat my tulip bulbs.

Or I can nurture a tree or a shrub or a bed with the tenderest care and still have it die for no apparent reason.

I can do everything right, in other words, but I cannot guarantee success.

The results are out of my hands.

That's why I've learned to think of our garden as a gift, despite the hard work that Bob and I (especially Bob) put into it. We can do our job as gardeners, but we cannot force good results. Still, the results in our garden so often are good, and that is a wonderful gift.

There is so much else my garden teaches. I've learned the value of good preparation and solid planning, of thinking ahead of the season and anticipating what is likely to happen. I use what I've learned as I fertilize the lawn ahead of coming rains, and as we contribute to our retirement programs.

But I've also learned to wait, which is a companion virtue. Even though I admit to being an impatient gardener, my garden has taught me many lessons in patience.

For me, the hardest part of gardening is the preparation. I get impatient with the processes of digging, fertilizing, preparing the beds. I tend to want instant flowers. But that's not the way it works, in the garden or in life.

If you want daffodils in March or April, you have to plant the bulbs in October or November. If you want climbing, curling sweet peas, you have to plant the seeds early and prepare the frames for them to climb on.

Even if you go to the garden center and buy three dozen pansy plants, you have to wait to get them

Flavorful Flowers

Did you know that you can eat flowers? Many of the blooms in your garden are gourmet delights! Here's a list of some of the most popular edible flowers and their flavors.

nasturtium—spicy

chives—oniony

squash, daylily—like a vegetable

calendula—buttery

mint, pansy—minty

sage, marigold—herbal

rose, violet—floral

home and planted, and before you do that you have to get their bed ready for them. And I really do want something besides pansies and mums in my garden. So I have to have patience. I have to do my job and then wait on the season, wait for the natural progression of growth.

I have to do that with the other growing issues of my life as well. When I try to break a bad habit or acquire a new one, when I try to mend a broken relationship or build a new friendship, I can't expect instant results. I must simply do what I know to do, then patiently wait for the results. My experience in the garden tells me that the results will probably be worthwhile—I'll either achieve my objective, or I'll learn something I needed to learn.

Pruning is another learning issue for me in the garden. On our property we have maybe three hundred trees of different varieties: fruit trees and shade trees, sycamores and ashes and pepper trees, even a beautiful olive tree. Every few years, Bob will call the tree trimmer, and I don't like to be there when it happens. Trimming always seems so brutal, like butchering the trees. Our fruitless mulberry trees are nothing but woody nubs when the trimmer is finished.

But as painful as the trimming process is, I have learned it pays big results. The trunks become stronger, and the foliage comes in lush and green. It always amazes me when those big branches and huge leaves come out from those pruned-back mulberries.

There are many situations in our garden that call for that kind of "tough love." We have to thin out a bed of seedlings, ripping out some so that others have a chance for life. If a plant doesn't work in one place, it must be moved, and we've sometimes had to discard a bush or a tree that just didn't look or grow right. And, of course, we must watch for weeds, sometimes sacrificing the life of one plant for another.

Effort
is only
troublesome
when you
are bored.

CHRISTOPHER
LLOYD

There have been many times when I've needed the pruning and thinning and weeding lesson in my own life. Sometimes I have had to weed out harmful activities that hurt my health or sapped my time and energy. Often I have had to thin out my schedule to make room for what I really want. And there have been a few times when I had to take out the pruning hook, making radical cutbacks in areas of my life that were unsightly or unnecessary or just leading in the wrong direction. Once or twice I have even had to prune back my life to the very basics, using this time of curtailment to store up my strength and remember who I am.

Now, I'll have to admit that I wasn't always the one imposing these disciplines on myself, at least not consciously. Sometimes life did it for me. But looking back, I can see it had to be done. I am trying to see the opportunities for pruning ahead of time and to make wiser decisions about what to pull and cut and hoe.

Pruning is just one of the many lessons my garden has taught me—some hard, some pure delight, many just instructive. I've learned hope, and joy, and wonder. I've learned about the value and rewards of work. I've learned volumes about the way things grow, about the way the world is structured, and now I'm learning ways to be more responsible for the world: conserving water, cutting back on pesticides, recycling wastes.

For the most part, I'm a happy pupil.

And what child ever had a more beautiful schoolroom?

The Joy of Journaling

"When did those miniature daffodils bloom last year? And how many did I order in the first place?"
"I thought these roses were a different color last summer."
"I wonder what would happen if we moved the little redbud over in that corner."
"And what is the meaning of life, anyway?"

In gardening and in life, the message is the same: If you want to learn it, write it down! The habit of keeping a garden journal can pay wonderful dividends from year to year. Not only will you have a record of what you planted where (seed packets quickly become weatherbeaten and illegible), but you will also have a place to jot down your brilliant ideas and warn yourself of mistakes you never want to make again.

Your journal doesn't have to be fancy; any simple notebook will do. And it doesn't have to be profound; doodles and scribbled notes can be as valuable to you as someone else's elegantly penned musings. You may even want to include pressed specimens or sample seed packets.

No matter how you keep your journal, you're bound to learn from it. And you'll be in good company. Famous garden journalists from the past include Thomas Jefferson and George Washington. Their careful records have been instrumental in teaching us about historical garden practices and in restoring estates such as Monticello and Mount Vernon to their original splendor.

Who knows?

Perhaps some future gardener will learn from reading what you put in your garden journal today.

Everything I Need to Know I Learned in My Garden

A Gathering of Acquired Wisdom for Inside and Outside the Garden Gate

Begin early. But it's never too late to start.

If it doesn't work, try something else.

Life is fragile. Protect it.

Life is enduring. Trust it.

Life is daily. Water it. Weed it. Prune it.

Life is indescribably beautiful. Enjoy it and say thank you.

Growth takes time. Be patient. And while you're waiting, pull a weed.

There's something for everybody— different blooms for different rooms.

Pruning hurts. Pruning helps you grow.

Recycle.

Sometimes the tiniest flowers smell the sweetest.

To everything there is a season. But know what zone you're in.

Dream big. But try not to let ambition turn your joy into drudgery.

Grow what you love. The love will keep it growing.

You reap what you sow. But there will be surprises!

A Healthful Harvest

Eating Well from Your Garden

What can compare to the fresh bounty from your garden—the fruits and vegetables and herbs and even the flowers? Unless you go out of your way to add calories and cholesterol, garden eating is healthy eating. As Bob and I have learned more about the ways of the garden, we have discovered delicious ways to enjoy our harvest. We've even learned that many flowers are edible and delicious!

Here's a gathering of luscious recipes I enjoy using. Unless otherwise indicated, herbs are dried (but home-dried herbs are infinitely superior to store-bought). As a rule of thumb, 1 tablespoon fresh or frozen herbs equals 1 teaspoon crushed dried herbs or ⅔ teaspoon powdered.

EMILIE'S FRESH TOMATO PASTA SAUCE WITH BASIL

> 1 tablespoon olive oil
> 12 fresh tomatoes, cut up
> (I leave the skin
> and seeds)
> 2 tablespoons fresh basil
> leaves, minced
> (or to taste)
> 4 or 5 garlic cloves, minced
> ½ teaspoon salt
> 2 tablespoons capers

Heat oil in deep frying pan, add all ingredients at once, and let simmer 10 to 15 minutes. Pour over hot angel-hair pasta.

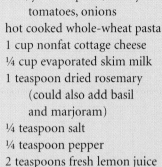

SUZANNE'S PASTA PRIMAVERA WITH ROSEMARY

> zucchini, yellow squash, cherry
> tomatoes, onions
> hot cooked whole-wheat pasta
> 1 cup nonfat cottage cheese
> ¼ cup evaporated skim milk
> 1 teaspoon dried rosemary
> (could also add basil
> and marjoram)
> ¼ teaspoon salt
> ¼ teaspoon pepper
> 2 teaspoons fresh lemon juice

Slice vegetables and saute in olive oil until tender-crisp; mix with pasta and keep warm. Blend together remaining ingredients and serve over pasta and vegetables. Don't heat; put over hot pasta to warm.

LEMON BAKED FISH

> 1 pound frozen fish fillet or
> steak
> 1¼ teaspoon Sue's Herb Fish
> Seasoning (see
> page 46)
> juice of 1 lemon (¼ cup)
> ½ small onion, thinly sliced

Microwave in its wrapper on full power for 2 to 3 minutes per pound. Loosen wrapper or make several slits in top of package. Thaw 1½ minutes. Remove wrapper, place on plate, re-cover, and complete thawing; let rest 10 minutes. Pour a bit of lemon juice in baking dish and arrange fish evenly in single layer; pour remaining lemon juice evenly over the top. Sprinkle fish with Sue's Herb Fish Seasoning and sliced onion. Cover and microwave on full power 5 to 7 minutes per pound, turning once if needed; let rest 5 minutes.

Or bake 20 to 30 minutes at 350 degrees, basting 2 or 3 times. Fish is done when it's opaque and flakes easily with a fork.

FROM SUE GREGG

SUE'S HERB FISH SEASONING

> 1 tablespoon onion powder
> 1 tablespoon dill
> 1 tablespoon garlic, powdered
> 1 tablespoon thyme leaves, crushed
> 1 tablespoon paprika
> 1 tablespoon dried parsley flakes

Thoroughly blend and store in refrigerator or freezer. Makes enough for 12 pounds of fish.

FROM SUE GREGG

UNCLE HY'S CORN

My uncle had a big garden where he loved to grow fresh corn for the sole purpose of his famous barbecues. I've never tasted anything like his barbecued corn, fresh from the garden and hot off the coals.

> Soak ears in the husk for a couple of hours in a bucket of water, then prepare the charcoal on the barbecue and put the corn on the grill and lower to the charcoal. Cook 20 to 30 minutes, turning every 10 minutes. (The outside will get charcoaly and burnt.) Then take the corn off the grill, pull off the husks, and inside will be the

most delicious, moist, steamed sweet corn you have ever eaten. Enjoy!

But the lesson I have thoroughly learnt, and wish to pass on to others, is to know the enduring happiness that the love of a garden gives. . . .
For love of gardening is a seed that once sown never dies, but always grows and grows to an enduring and ever-increasing source of happiness. . . .
Each new step becomes a little surer, and each new grasp a little firmer, till, little by little, comes the power of intelligent combination, the nearest thing we know to the mighty force of creation.

GERTRUDE JEKYLL

HERB AND FLOWER SALAD

> 6 cups mixed baby greens
> > 1 cup green leaf herbs (basil, tarragon, Italian parsley, chervil)
> ½ cup edible petals (see sidebar on page 41)

Toss greens and herbs together and arrange the edible petals on top for a decorative look. Toss at the table with Emilie's Olive Oil Dressing.

EMILIE'S OLIVE OIL DRESSING

(My Viennese-chef father, Otto, taught me this recipe. Gets compliments every time!)
MAKES: 1½ cups
Mash together and put in a jar:
3 cloves garlic, pressed
> 1 teaspoon salt
> ½ scant teaspoon pepper
Add and shake well:
> 1 cup olive oil
> ½ cup wine vinegar
> juice of 1 lemon (about ¼ cup)
Chill before spooning over salad greens.

PARMESAN DILL BREAD

> ½ cup warm water
> 1 tablespoon (1 package) active dry yeast
> 1 tablespoon honey
> ⅛ teaspoon vitamin C powder (optional, to assist rising)

2 cups hot water
2 teaspoons salt
⅓ cup honey
⅓ cup vegetable oil (light
olive or canola
preferred)
6 cups whole-wheat flour
4 tablespoons Parmesan
cheese
1 to 2 teaspoons dill seeds
1 egg beaten with water
dill seeds for garnish

Pour ½ cup very warm (not hot)
water in a glass measuring cup.
Add yeast, 1 tablespoon honey, and
vitamin C powder (in that order)
and allow to stand 5 to 10 minutes
until it bubbles up. In mixing bowl,
blend hot water, salt, ⅓ cup honey,
and vegetable oil. Mix in 3 cups
flour, then yeast mixture. Stir in as
much of the next 3 cups of flour as
you can until stirring becomes difficult, then turn dough out on a
floured surface to knead in the
remaining flour. Knead for 10
minutes, adding flour as needed to
prevent sticking, but using as little
flour over the basic 6 cups as you
can. Place dough in lightly oiled
bowl, oil top of dough lightly, cover
with a cloth, and let rise in a warm
place until double in size, about 1
to 1½ hours. Punch dough down.
Now you're ready to shape into Dill
loaves.

To shape, divide dough
into 2 equal pieces. Pat each piece
of dough into a rectangle about ½"

thick, then cut each rectangle into 3
equal pieces with a table knife
dipped in water. Sprinkle each piece
not quite to the edges with half of
the cheese and dill seeds. Roll up
each piece from the long side; pinch
edge to seal the roll, and braid the
three rolled strips together. (Don't
worry if braid is longer than the
pan. You can shorten it as you lift it
into the pan.) Place loaves in
greased pans and brush tops with
beaten egg or water (for shiny crust)
and sprinkle dill seeds over the top.
Let rise and bake at 350 degrees for
35 minutes. Makes 2 medium loaves.
FROM SUE GREGG

HEALTHY HERB BUTTER SPREAD

4 ounces (½ stick or ¼
cup) lightly salted
butter, very soft
¼ cup canola oil
1½ teaspoons liquid
lecithin (optional)
2 teaspoons fresh lemon
juice
1 tablespoon fresh parsley,
chopped
1 tablespoon fresh basil (or 2
teaspoons dried herbs)

Combine butter, lecithin, and lemon
juice in oil. Gradually beat oil mixture until smooth, with no lumps.
Vary herbs according to taste—
try lime with chives, summer
savory and onion powder, or
Italian seasoning.
ADAPTED FROM EATING RIGHT

Hand in hand with fairy grace
Will we sing, and bless this place.

William Shakespeare

A Time for Wonder

Why Children Grow in My Garden, Too

It was one of those early autumn afternoons when everything seems perfect: impossibly blue sky, light breeze, golden sun that had lost a bit of its summer edge. Here in southern California, the leaves don't turn brilliant colors, but the flowers continue much longer. We still had rafts of roses blooming along with the chrysanthemums. The sunflowers were still bright back behind the vegetables, and the avocado trees were heavy with fruit.

Papa Bob and our grandson Bevan, then about five, had spent an hour or two in the vegetable garden, picking tomatoes and eggplant, pulling out the occasional weed that managed to stick its head above the mulch, tidying up some of the overgrown foliage from a bumper summer's crop. Then they had gone out into the grove and gathered a basket of oranges and lemons and avocados.

Now the basket rested at their feet as they sat on the bench out under the avocado tree, their look-alike faces echoing the same satisfaction of work well done. I saw them through my kitchen window and prepared a tray of cold lemonade to take to them. As I drew near, I heard Bob say to Bevan with a touch of pride in his voice, "You know, Bevan, someday when you're a grown man you'll drive down Rumsey Drive and look at all this and remember all the good work we did here in our garden."

"Yeah!" agreed Bevan. He was quiet just a minute, then he added thoughtfully, "And when I bring my grandson by, he'll remember, too."

At age five, Bevan had already discovered a bedrock truth about gardens.

Not only are they wonderful places for children to grow. They are also unmatched for leaving a legacy of beauty and strength and meaningful work for our children and our grandchildren and our children's grandchildren.

I must admit, in fact, that a good part of our gardening is done for the sake of our grandchildren. Both Bob and I are teachers at heart, and as we have evolved from parents into grandparents we have become far more conscious of the importance of the green legacy we can leave behind.

When our own children were small, we lived in suburban tract homes with typical yards. The children were always expected to help in the yard, and both have become involved with the gifts of the garden in their own ways as adults. But it is their children who have been intimately involved with our garden almost since birth.

When Christine and Chad and Bevan and little Bradley Joe and now little Weston were infants, we loved to take them out in the garden and show them things—hold them up to a flower for a sniff, point out the singing birds, the tall trees. As they began to toddle and explore, we encouraged them to dig in the dirt, to make mud pies, to "pick the pretty flower"—under supervision, of course. It wasn't long until they were out in the vegetable garden "helping" Bob water seedlings, pull weeds, trim back growing plants. They were walking with me out to make bouquets, taking a cool drink to Papa Bob, being rewarded with "I was caught being good"

To pick a flower is so much more satisfying than just observing it, or photographing it.... So in later years I have grown in my garden as many flowers as possible for children to pick.

ANNE SCOTT-JAMES

stickers. They especially loved to help with harvesting. They would fill a little basket with green beans, carrots, or radishes, bring the basket in to Grammy, and we'd fill the sink to wash the vegetables, eating as we went.

You can imagine how delighted those children were when Bob set aside a little plot of ground for each of them and let them choose what to plant. Sometimes they would grow vegetables, sometimes flowers—we always let them choose. And they were always proudest of the harvest from "my garden."

It's no secret that children and gardens just naturally go together. The garden is outside in the fresh air, and so much is going on there. In fact, the garden is a completely stocked science lab where even the tiniest child can begin learning the basics of botany, biology, even chemistry. They learn that tiny seeds can grow into big trees, that plants make food in their leaves and drink through their roots, that flowers, like children, need food and drink and sunlight and love.

Children are natural observers, and they learn so much more when they can see what they're learning. In fact, I've found that children see so much more than adults do, perhaps because they're closer to the ground, perhaps because they look at the world through fresh eyes. So many of our walks have been brightened because one of the children spotted an unusual bug under a leaf or a fairy-sized flower in the wildflower meadow. Such discoveries build camaraderie and makes sharing easier.

Working together is a great way to build relationships—there's something about the rhythm of digging and weeding that makes sharing more natural and coaxes out confidences. It's also a great way of teaching responsibility and natural consequences. The kids get to see firsthand what happens if you start something and don't finish it or if you neglect something you're responsible for. More often, though, the lesson is a positive one. Work becomes much more meaningful (even fun) for kids when it brings tangible rewards such as fresh vegetables and flowers. Our grandchildren love to pick their own dinner, bringing in the fruits and vegetables for me to wash and cook. And they are far more motivated to eat the right kind of food when they had a hand in growing it.

Most of the time, of course, children don't really realize they're "working" in the garden. Up to a certain age, at least, garden work is fun. And our grandchildren help us remember that, too. The more time we spend with them in the garden, the more fun we have, too.

One of our most fun projects, quite a few years ago now, was the Great Pumpkin Factory. Christine and Chad were small at the time, Bevan was a baby, and Bradley Joe and Weston were not yet a twinkle in anyone's eye. Bob has always loved autumn, and he decided it would be fun to have some pumpkins in October. So he bought one small package of pumpkin seeds, took the kids out to the garden, built up a little hill of soil, and let each child plant a handful of seeds. Every time they came over they would have to go out and water their vines and see how the pumpkins were growing. And did those pumpkins grow! Vines spread everywhere, and soon we could see little green pumpkins beginning to swell.

You've probably guessed the rest of the story. Out of that one package of seeds we harvested sixty pumpkins. We were famous all over town! We had pumpkins out by the mailbox, pumpkins next to the garden bench, pumpkins stacked by the front door. I learned to make pumpkin bread and pumpkin muffins and to serve pumpkin soup in a pumpkin-shell bowl. Christine's preschool class came over, and each child picked a pumpkin to take home. A lady in our neighborhood who admired all our pumpkins dropped by to say she had been by a local pumpkin patch to see about getting that many pumpkins for her yard. She learned there was no way she could afford so many.

That year was a once-in-a-lifetime pumpkin harvest. Never again have we been able to grow that many in a season. But what a wonderful experience for our little ones—to see their little beginnings produce such a glorious result!

We've had such wonderful times with the children in our garden. I've written many times of the birthday tea parties Christine and I have shared for many years. Those special and beautiful times, complete with a handpicked bouquet from our garden, are precious to both Christine and Grammy. But we've had special garden parties for the boys, too. Especially memorable was the Operation Desert Storm cookout we held for Chad and Bevan. This was during the Persian Gulf War. All the guests wore camouflage. They played around the property, then went into the garden to pick the vegetables for the cookout. Zucchini, yellow squash, corn, tomatoes—all were washed, seasoned, wrapped in foil, and put on the grill, along with juicy hamburgers and chicken. Everything we ate we cooked outside. . . and then ate on tin pie plates.

Much later, when little Bradley Joe turned two, we turned our garden into a petting zoo. We discovered that a couple who live just about ten miles from town would bring the zoo to us. They came in a pickup truck, set up a chainlink fence around a twelve by fifteen foot area, and brought in a regular Noah's ark of animals for the children to touch and enjoy. Our garden was full of goats, chickens, piglets, ducks, a calf, and a pony—all separated, of course, from the vulnerable plants! The children were given feed for the animals and brushes for grooming. The adults got in and lay on the grass with the children around them and let the little animals come up and nibble on their ears and necks. The piglets would climb in our laps and fall asleep. That, too, was a wonderful time of fun in our garden.

Children bring so much extra life, so much meaning to a garden! If there are no children currently growing in your garden, I urge you to borrow some! Invite a young family from church to come over for a picnic. Talk to neighborhood children and invite them in, explaining clearly what they should not do and what they are welcome to do. (They must knock on the door and let you know they're there. They must not trample the flower beds. They must not pick or eat anything without checking with you first.)

And take the time to make your garden more child-friendly.

First of all, be safety conscious. Never leave sharp tools lying around, and don't leave small children unsupervised. Be especially careful about pools and ponds, because children can drown in just a few seconds. (If you have toddlers, you may want to hold off on that fish pond for a year or two.) If you use pesticides and herbicides, make sure they are stored in locked cabinets and in their original containers—never in soda bottles.

But it is the efforts you make beyond these basic safety considerations that will make your garden inviting for children. When you choose what to plant, think on a small scale as well as on your own larger, adult scale. Plant tiny plants in tiny corners, ready for small eyes to discover. Plant at least a few sturdy flowers and trees that rambunctious children cannot easily harm. And be sure to plant some berries or other "pick right off the vine and eat" (after washing) delights.

A child-friendly garden will have special places for children to play. Children love cozy nooks and crannies, and with a little planning such spots are easy to arrange in any garden. We have a wonderful tree house that serves as a fort, a castle, a ship, a teahouse—whatever it's called upon to do. It's perched in a majestic, seventy-five-year-old shamel ash tree and has a slide coming down. Our grandchildren also enjoy playing in those heavy-duty commercial plastic toy houses, which we can nestle out beneath the trees. But you don't really need a specially constructed playhouse. A little trellised arch covered with grapevines or wisteria can serve the same purpose. So can a circle of hedges, carefully trimmed, or a weeping willow tree whose branches curve gently down to the ground.

Our friend Ellen, who helps us so much in our business, for many years has planted grapevines for the express purpose of giving her children hiding places. She plants them about four feet from their garden wall and then trains them toward the wall on wires, leaving a leafy little nook between the base of the vines and the fence. The vines grow fast and quickly enclose the area, and her children love climbing among them. (When Ellen's house and garden were new, she found the grapevine playhouse invaluable in protecting her tender young trees from intrepid little climbers.)

The children themselves will be ingenious in finding hiding places. (You may find, when the children aren't home, that you love to curl up in a "hidey-hole" yourself!)

Yet another way to make a garden child-friendly is to make areas of it special to them. This can start as soon as they are born—or even before! When you are expecting, plant something in the baby's honor: a row of corn, a rosebush, a perennial plot. Then as the baby grows you can point out this special spot. Children may not understand all the implications, but they will be able to understand that they are a part of what is happening in the garden.

Later, when the children reach preschool age, let them have a garden spot to call their own. Buy each child a little shovel and trowel. Then help him or her prepare a very small bed (about fifteen by twelve inches square). Mark off the area, turn the soil, add manure—do whatever you do in your larger garden. Go on a walk together to find stones to lay around the edge, then let the child plant whatever he or she wants out of what you're planting: a tomato plant, some nasturtium seeds, a bunch of sunflowers. Big seeds are usually easier for little fingers to handle. And be sure and plant some extra, because there will be a strong temptation to dig up the seeds to see how they're doing.

Whenever you're out working in your garden, take the children with you and show them what you are doing—weeding, fertilizing, watering, checking for bugs, whatever. Help them if they need it, but let them make the decisions—even those that may not work. My friend Ellen has been doing this with her children since they were tiny. The children loved it! They learned from their successes and mistakes. (One creative son decided to transplant everything in the garden somewhere else!) They also had something to do while Mom was out in the yard. And the whole family enjoyed seeing what came up in the kids' gardens.

It doesn't take much work to make a garden child-friendly because gardens are inherently child-friendly. And bringing children into your garden experience pays such big rewards. Children help you learn. They freshen your wonder. And as they pass on the learning and the wonder to their own children and grandchildren, they become a longer-lasting legacy than any tree or bush or flower you could ever grow.

Worms and Ladybugs

A Garden Party for the Young at Heart

This is a fun way to celebrate the birthday of a favorite youngster, especially one who likes to help in the garden. Or have a party like this anytime, adjusting the activities to the age, gender, and activity level of the party-goers. You can have a quiet, ladylike "garden tea party" with dress-up clothes, pretty bouquets, and lots of flowers. Or you can ask guests to wear overalls or shorts for a more casual approach. This party can be adapted for indoors or outdoors, using either fresh plants and flowers from your garden or silk and paper ones from your own creative hands.

INVITATIONS: Glue an inexpensive packet of seeds to a large index card and write in party information above the packet. Be sure and specify whether it's an indoor or outdoor party and what the guests are supposed to wear.

DECORATIONS: For serving, use a picnic table or patio table covered with bright floral sheets or vinyl cloths (available from a fabric store). A table with an umbrella makes an especially pretty setting—you can decorate the edges of the umbrella with garlands of ivy, sweet pea, or other vines, and wind a vine up the central pole. (Secure with pins and florist's tape.) Awnings, porch posts, and so on, can be similarly adorned, and place flowers everywhere (real, silk, paper). Spread more sheets or vinyl squares on the ground for a picnic, or decorate additional tables for sitting.

A little red wagon or galvanized tub filled with potted plants makes a fun centerpiece—or place it to the side as a decoration.

REFRESHMENTS: Use your imagination in serving the refreshments. A plastic watering can makes an imaginative lemonade pitcher. Veggies can be cut into long slices and served in tiny clay flowerpots. Dip in a plastic container can be tucked into another clay pot or into a hollowed-out red cabbage.

*Garden Patch Cake with ice cream
lemonade with mint leaves
veggie tray with Garden Dip
jelly gems (jelly sandwiches cut
in fancy shapes)
sunflower seeds*

GARDEN PATCH CAKE

sheet cake (any kind)—1 layer
chocolate frosting
vanilla sugar wafers, long oval
    sandwich cookies, or
    other long cookies or
    crackers
chocolate sandwich cookies,
    crumbled
small flowers (violets, Johnny-
    jump-ups, nastur-
    tiums, daisies)
mint leaves (or sugar leaves)
small soda straws or coffee
    stirrers (green or
    white)
gummy worms

Frost cake with chocolate frosting. Place cookies around edge of cake like a fence, with the edges sticking up. Gently press dental floss horizontally and vertically across cake to mark it into serving-sized squares; use a leaf tip to pipe green frosting around the edge of each square (on either side of floss) and around inside edge of "fence." Carefully spread cookie crumbs inside of squares to simulate dirt. Cut straws or stirrers into 2" lengths and insert in center of squares, leaving about an inch above the surface; these will be the stems of your flowers. Place mint leaves or sugar leaves around base of straw or glue on tiny paper leaves. Remove strands of dental floss and position a few gummy worms here and there on the cake. If you wish, use green food coloring to tint coconut and the place around the base of the cake, then lay another gummy worm and a few extra blossoms here and there. If desired, serve with a scoop of green mint ice cream. If you use edible flowers such as Johnny-jump-ups or nasturtiums, tell the children they can eat their flowers! This will be a big hit among boys. But warn them about going around and tasting flowers indiscriminately (some may be covered with pesticides, others are poisonous).

GARDEN DIP
Most children will be happier with a very mild ranch or thousand island dressing. For older children, mix one part plain yogurt with one part sour cream. Then add green and red pepper chopped finely, garlic powder, and chives.

Activities
PIN THE BEE ON THE BLOSSOM:
Paint a big piece of poster board (at least twenty-four inches by thirty-six inches) with a very large, off-center rose. Fill rest of design with winding stems, rosebuds, and leaves. Draw at least

Our children have grown with the garden; every niche has been nursery, governess, and playmate.... My garden has been a pirate ship, Barbie Doll vacation paradise, Sylvanian Family campground, jungle, maze, obstacle course, arena for birthday treasure hunts, and the Yukon for Calvin and Hobbes. It is well peopled.

SANDY PUCKETT

five or six bees with a black marker on yellow self-stick adhesive pads, making sure the design includes part of the adhesive section. (You can also find pull-off adhesive "glue" at office supply stores.) Cut out bees. Blindfold children with floral fabric and have them take turns trying to stick the bee on the large rose.

WORM AND LADYBUG RELAY: Divide children into teams and divide each team into an equal number of "worms" and "ladybugs." For each team, mark start and finish lines about 12 feet apart. Line up worms at the start lines and ladybugs at the finish lines. When you say "go," the first worm must crawl on his stomach (no hands!) all the way to his ladybug teammate. When the worm's head crosses the line, the first ladybug spreads out her arms and flies away home—all the way back to the worm line. She tags the first worm in line, who starts out crawling again. The first team to exchange worms and ladybugs wins. If you want to, play again so that each child gets to be a worm and a ladybug. (Note: If you play this outside, you may want to have the worms crawl on strips of tarp or plastic to protect their clothes from grass stains.)

GARDEN BEANBAG TOSS: Sew up beanbags in a variety of garden fabrics, or get creative and make sunflower beanbags or daisy beanbags and so on (sew circle and surround with fabric "petals"). Have children take turns tossing beanbags into a nest of galvanized washtubs. Those who hit the center tub get ten points, and the outer tub get five points.

Or try playing with large clay flowerpots, hula hoops, trellises, or whatever you can think of. Give simple, garden-related prizes.

LADYBUG LIBERATION: Order ladybugs from a garden supply catalog and let party-goers release them all around your garden.

SECRET GARDEN PARTY: For an indoor party when the weather is less than perfect, why not show *The Secret Garden* on video?

PICTURE BOOKS IN THE GARDEN: Gather together young children for a story time and read the tale of Peter Rabbit or other Beatrix Potter stories. Talk about where Peter and his friends might hide in your house and garden.

THE GARDEN PLOT: Buy small green socks and help the children glue on bright flower and vegetable faces made out of felt. Try to have happy faces, sad faces, angry faces. If you buy white, gray, and brown socks, they can make bunnies, squirrels, and other garden animals. (If one child is determined to make King Kong, just compliment her creativity and talk about what King Kong might do in a garden.) Then have them make up a garden play. You can also make flower stick puppets out of paper and Popsicle sticks.

SCAVENGER HUNT: Send groups of kids out in your garden or through the neighborhood to find certain items: a heart-shaped leaf, a moth, a packet of seeds, a watering can, a pair of clippers. (It's best to send a chaper-

one with each group.) Be sure to have them return all the items at the end of the party. Or have an instant-camera scavenger hunt. Send groups out with an instant camera to take pictures of the items they found.

Even if she forgets the whole thing in her teens, later still, when she is grown up and has a first garden of her own, some misty memory of the pleasure of growing things will give her a headstart over the gardener without any background, just as children who have spoken a second language, and forgotten it, can pick it up again in later years.

ANNE
SCOTT-
JAMES

Make Your Own Favors

GARDEN CUPS: Have a small Mason jar or stadium cup for every guest. As guests arrive, let each one draw a garden design on his or her cup with paint pens. Children can drink their lemonade or punch in their cups and then take them home as favors. (I did this once for a party of five-year-old boys. Years later the mother of one of my guests told me he still had his cup and liked to drink from it.)

GARDEN HATS: Purchase straw hats, cloth "gimme" hats, or plastic visors and let each guest decorate his or her own. Supply fabric paints, craft glue, ribbons, bunches of dried or silk flowers, buttons, and novelty items such as fuzzy bees and silk butterflies. For a small group or older children, you can provide a glue gun to help them decorate, but supervise carefully. (You keep the gun!)

PAINTED FLOWERPOTS: Carefully wash small 3½" clay pots and let them dry. Provide party-goers with acrylic craft paints, brushes, newspapers, and smocks (old T-shirts work fine) to decorate their pots. Do this at the beginning of the party so pots can dry during refreshment time. Send guests home with a Ziploc bag of potting soil, a small packet of seeds, and instructions for planting—or tell them to use the seeds they received with the invitation.

Garden Play
Eight Child-Friendly Activities

• **A THUMBELINA TEA PARTY:** Find a tiny nook in the garden, spread a clean, lace-edged handkerchief, and lay out a miniature feast with either a toy tea set or makeshift dishes (try acorn cups, leaves, twigs). Use pretend food, or set out tiny morsels (cookie crumbs, raisin slices, and so forth). Once the table is set, pretend to invite Thumbelina to tea while you read her story aloud.

• **A FAIRY'S BOUQUET:** My friend Bill Jensen loves to take his two little girls around their garden in the early morning and help them pick fairy bouquets. They gather miniature roses, linaria, violets, honeysuckle—whatever tiny flowers or parts of flowers will fit the scale. Then they tie slender ribbons around the little nosegays and pop them into pill bottles, spice bottles, or miniature bud vases. The girls love to have their little bouquets next to their breakfast plates.

• **FLOWER GAMES:** Do you remember little games you used to play with flowers and plants as a child? Could you find the bead of nectar at the base of a honeysuckle blossom, fashion clover or daisy chains, "snap" snapdragons, or make ladies out of hollyhock blossoms? Remember to teach these to your children while you're walking in the garden. Every child loves to find the faces in a bed of pansies.

• **LITTLE CRITTER SAFARI:** Take a piece of dark paper and a magnifying glass and go on a hunting trip together. Look under leaves, pick through the grass, and even dig in the dirt and see what you can find. Shake a plant gently over the paper and look at what falls off. Talk about which critters are helpful (earthworms, ladybugs, praying mantises, most spiders) and which are harmful (aphids, snails, tomato hornworms). If you don't know much about insects yourself, take along a child's nature book and learn together.

• **A TREE FOR ME:** Go to the garden center and let each child pick out a tree to be planted in his or her honor. Make a ceremony of planting it at home, at the child's school, or at church. Your children will love to watch the progress of the tree as it grows—and they grow with it.

• **PRESSING FLOWERS:** Older children will enjoy learning to press flowers and leaves from the garden and arranging them into graceful pictures. Press flowers between pages of an old phone book or between layers of newspaper under a heavy weight. When the flowers are completely dry (after several weeks), use tweezers and a tiny bit of white glue to arrange them and add accents of lace and ribbon, if desired. If you wish, cover carefully with clear adhesive paper to protect the fragile flowers.

• **A WORM'S-EYE VIEW:** Fill a gallon glass jar with alternate layers of soil and sand. Add leaf mold, coffee grounds, bits of banana peel, and other compost matter. Place the jar on a shelf in a cabinet or half cover with black cloth or paper. Add about ten worms. From time to time remove the black paper for short intervals to see how the worms work and live. After a month or so, release them back in the garden.

• **A SUNFLOWER HOUSE:** Plant four giant sunflowers in a square, about four feet apart. Once the sunflowers are about a foot tall, plant morning glories around the base of each flower. The morning glory vines will climb up around the sunflowers. Then, when the flowers reach six feet or so, tie a web of strings across the space between the sunflowers. Coax the morning glories to twine across the strings and form a room. The resulting sunflower house won't last forever, but it will be wonderful fun in the meantime.

Rise up, my love, my fair one, and come away.

For, lo, the winter is past, the rain is over and gone.

The flowers appear on the earth;

the time of the singing of birds is come,

and the voice of the turtle is heard in our land.

Song of Solomon 2:10-12

A Time for Romance

The Spice of a Well-Lived Life

ong before the floral shops told us to "say it with flowers," the language of the garden has been the language of romance.

The single, perfect rose.

The moonlit, honeysuckle-scented walk.

The white daisy that answers the yearning question, "Does he love me?"

The creamy-white bridal bouquet.

Who can resist such wonderful, breathless words? All of them whisper, "You are beautiful. You are special. You are alive."

And I don't think you should resist.

Surely everyone needs a little romance in his or her life.

In today's world we often have trouble understanding romance and its proper place in the overall scheme of things.

On one hand, we elevate romance to the place of highest importance.

We equate it with love, with beauty. We promote the myth that human beings can't live without romance, and that romance is the highest human aim.

Or we grow suspicious of romance, label it a lie, tell ourselves we're better off without it. We celebrate being tough, clearheaded, reality-based, and we shy suspiciously away from any hint of the sentimental. We think we're safer that way. We think we're cool, sophisticated.

But I don't think we need to go to the extremes of either living for romance or coldly living without it.

I like to think of romance as a wonderful flowering herb that adds beauty and fragrance and excitement to my life. It makes my meals more flavorful, my work more enjoyable, my leisure more pleasurable.

Romance is not the same thing as love or character or spiritual integrity. We don't really need romance to survive. But a touch of romance can make our lives and relationships so much more pleasant, so much richer and more beautiful.

Romance is the spice of a well-lived life, the spark in a loving relationship. It is beauty, excitement, sensual pleasure, freshness, and delight. Romance makes you feel larger than life, out of the ordinary, one of a kind. It can be adventurous and playful, intimate yet mysterious. Romance is fed by beauty, stimulated by risk.

> In his garden every man may be his own artist without apology or explanation. Here is one spot where each may experience the "romance of possibility."
>
> LOUISE BEEBE WILDER

Small wonder that the rose, with its sweet breath and prickly thorns, has so long been considered the epitome of romance! And small wonder that the garden aids and abets the romantic impulse so effectively.

Think of a meeting in the starlight by a splashing fountain. Think of the sweetness of night-blooming moonflowers mingling with the richness of damp earth. Think of a thin floral frock and a shady straw hat, a kiss under the arbor or a solitary seat and a book of poems.

Or think of a rose carefully nurtured and lovingly presented, a dish prepared from hand-grown herbs and tomatoes, a bouquet arranged with the greatest of care.

A garden gift is not less romantic for being carefully planned and thoughtfully prepared. Most people I know would consider such a gesture *more* romantic.

Romance tends to heighten the intensity of perception, and this fact may tie it even closer to the garden. Have you ever noticed how much brighter the sunshine seems to be when you are in love? How much happier your happiness, how intense your pain? Surely a garden is more beautiful as well... and perhaps the beauty of a garden echoes the effect, making the romantic feelings more intense.

Romance is also intensely personal. It twines around personal qualities and preferences, rejoices in the specific and the particular. Not just flowers—but columbines and asters and poppies and roses. Not just birds, but finches and bluebirds and grackles. The most romantic gestures are the ones that say clearly, "I see you. I hear you. I understand you. And I think you are beautiful." And very romantic people often develop "signature" flowers and plants (a rose, a violet, a sunflower) that proclaim their individuality.

The language of romance will be a little different for every individual. And that's important to note, because it's easy to become limited in our thinking about what is romantic. We think only of hearts and flowers, only of pink satin and lace, only of teenagers. We make assumptions that romance excludes good sense or practicality. But romance can be so much richer, so much broader than our circumscribed ideas.

For instance, it's perfectly possible to be romantic without being involved in a relationship—or hopelessly frustrated because one is not in a relationship. The language of romance does not necessarily require a dialogue. Anyone can add freshness and excitement to their environment; anyone can enjoy the element of romance in their life.

I think of single friends who surround themselves with beauty, who engage themselves fully in life, who enjoy the messages their senses bring them. Many of these are very romantic people. A person who dares to try something new, who makes the choice to work at what she loves, who makes the time for little gestures of beauty and grace may speak the language of romance more fluently than someone enmeshed in a dull, self-satisfied relationship.

And yet romance can certainly be a vital spark in a loving relationship. Often it's the impetus for getting started, the energy that compels us to draw closer and learn more about one another. If carefully nurtured over the life of a relationship, romance can enhance the quality of a couple's life for many years to come. The romantic garden is a perfect resource for that kind of nurturing.

When Bob and I were first dating, his funds were very limited. Roses were normally out of his reach, but he would often bring me a gift of a single carnation: red, pink, or "peppermint." Those simple little gifts meant so much to me because I knew what they were saying. They told me, "You are worth a flower." Some people think of carnations as ordinary, but to me they are still extraordinary romantic messengers. (Other women have told me they feel the same way about the ruffly, spicy-smelling flowers that bring back so many memories of young, fresh romance.)

Even more special and romantic to me are my Valentine sweet peas. One Valentine's Day my Bob planted me a whole row of sweet peas and even prepared a frame for them to twine on. He knew that ever since I was a little girl, I have adored sweet peas for their delicacy and their scent. Now we always have sweet peas in our garden, and every time I walk into the garden and sniff that delicious fragrance or gather a bouquet of delicate sweet peas for my windowsill, I receive a fresh reminder of the trouble Bob takes to make me feel special. How can romance help but bloom in such a climate?

We have found, in fact, that our romance buds brighter these days, with our kids grown and away from home, than it did even in the early days of our relationship. It doesn't have the same breathless, heartsick quality, but it thrives on shared experiences of beauty, shared enjoyments.

For instance, we love to share our "yellow rose." Bob comes from a long line of Texans. So quite a few years ago, when our yellow roses first got established, he began the practice of picking a "yellow rose of Texas" when he comes inside. "Here's your yellow rose of Texas," he tells me, handing it over with a bit of ceremony. And I take it and thank him with a kiss, and then either place it in a little vase or lay it gently on top of a bowl of potpourri. The roses from that lovely bush keep their shape beautifully and smell wonderful, so every time I catch a whiff of that rosy fragrance I have another reminder that romance is still alive in our lives.

Of course, I often use the garden to express my love to Bob as well. And yes, I have sent him flowers. I often pick a special bouquet and place it on his nightstand to enjoy—and I have learned that such gestures really make a difference to him. I use the herbs from the garden to prepare healthful and delicious meals for him, and we love to enjoy them out on the patio, where the fountain sparkles and the strawberries bloom. And from time to time I will give him a birdhouse or a new kind of rosebush or a beautiful garden book or even a new hoe or trowel. Because he loves nothing better than to be in the garden, these gifts are very personal expressions of my love to him.

Romantic giving from the garden can take so many shapes. Our friend Ellen does it by planting cacti for her husband, who hates gardening but loves cacti. She remembers a time when she planted a pot of cacti for him on the patio and then called him out to look. What a sweet, romantic gesture.

But romance is so much more than the giving of gifts. Romance thrives in beautiful, quiet settings like the garden, where there is time to enjoy one another away from everyday distractions. Bob and I love nothing better than to wander hand in hand through our garden in the early evening, talking quietly, breathing in the achingly beautiful fragrance of earth and orange and honeysuckle blossoms, looking over the place of beauty we have built together with love and tears and hard work. The air is gentle and soft and quiet. The excitement of being near one another mingles with the comfort of feeling safe and cherished.

In these times we don't have to say it with flowers.

The flowers say it for us.

And the language of that romantic conversation is also the language of our enduring love.

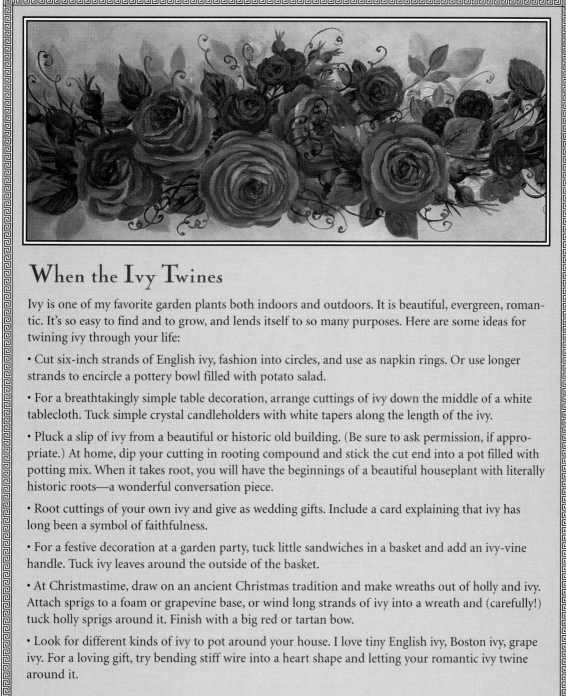

When the Ivy Twines

Ivy is one of my favorite garden plants both indoors and outdoors. It is beautiful, evergreen, romantic. It's so easy to find and to grow, and lends itself to so many purposes. Here are some ideas for twining ivy through your life:

• Cut six-inch strands of English ivy, fashion into circles, and use as napkin rings. Or use longer strands to encircle a pottery bowl filled with potato salad.

• For a breathtakingly simple table decoration, arrange cuttings of ivy down the middle of a white tablecloth. Tuck simple crystal candleholders with white tapers along the length of the ivy.

• Pluck a slip of ivy from a beautiful or historic old building. (Be sure to ask permission, if appropriate.) At home, dip your cutting in rooting compound and stick the cut end into a pot filled with potting mix. When it takes root, you will have the beginnings of a beautiful houseplant with literally historic roots—a wonderful conversation piece.

• Root cuttings of your own ivy and give as wedding gifts. Include a card explaining that ivy has long been a symbol of faithfulness.

• For a festive decoration at a garden party, tuck little sandwiches in a basket and add an ivy-vine handle. Tuck ivy leaves around the outside of the basket.

• At Christmastime, draw on an ancient Christmas tradition and make wreaths out of holly and ivy. Attach sprigs to a foam or grapevine base, or wind long strands of ivy into a wreath and (carefully!) tuck holly sprigs around it. Finish with a big red or tartan bow.

• Look for different kinds of ivy to pot around your house. I love tiny English ivy, Boston ivy, grape ivy. For a loving gift, try bending stiff wire into a heart shape and letting your romantic ivy twine around it.

Do You Speak Romance?

The Traditional Language of Flowers

From earliest times, flowers have carried symbolic meanings, often tied to their physical appearance or to myths and legends. Thus laurel, used to crown Greek heroes, became symbolic of glory, and the white lily, in its pristine beauty, came to be associated with the Virgin Mary and to represent purity. Shakespeare was well acquainted with the language of flowers, and many a poet from Elizabethan times on drew on the symbolism of the garden. Of course, lovers have always expressed their most tender sentiments with bouquets and floral offerings.

In the eighteenth and nineteenth centuries, however, the language of flowers developed into the most elaborate and specific of tongues. Different flowers became associated with different sentiments, and various combinations and means of presentation told a far more complex tale. Both givers and receivers were expected to be conversant in the romantic language of flowers. Unfortunately, the specific meanings sometimes varied from source to source—resulting, no doubt, in misunderstandings and even broken relationships.

There's rosemary, that's for remembrance; pray you, love, remember. And there is pansies, that's for thoughts.... There's fennel for you, and columbines. There's rue for you; and her; some for me. We may call it herb of grace a Sundays. O, you must wear your rue with a difference. There's a daisy. I would give you some violets, but they wither'd all...

WILLIAM SHAKESPEARE

Today, the language of flowers can be a fun resource for conveying romantic and friendly sentiments, although you will doubtless have to translate your message. A pressed pansy arranged on a simple blank note card can say "I'm thinking of you." A miniature basket of dried globe amaranths and baby's breath could carry a card that says "My love for you is everlasting." Why not give bouquets or corsages or boutonnieres that carry a special message as well?

Here is a dictionary of some of the most common flowers and their traditional meanings. Have fun with them, but also take them with a grain of salt. Remember that the sources vary and that your personal associations can be far more romantic than the traditional meanings. For me, a "yellow rose of Texas" will never carry the traditional message of "love is waning"!

Suzanne Fruitig Bales puts it this way: "Forget the symbols of flowers that represent unhappy, nasty, and hateful sentiments. The world has enough of those, and flowers are not the proper vehicle to express them. As many of these flowers are beautiful, group them into bouquets for a gallant gesture.... Remember that simplicity and sincerity are also necessary ingredients."

FLOWER	TRADITIONAL MEANING	FLOWER	TRADITIONAL MEANING
apple blossom	preference	nasturtium	patriotism
azalea	temperance	pansy	thinking of you, "think of me"
bachelor's button	single blessedness		
bluebell	constancy	petunia	never despair
camellia	perfected loveliness	phlox	unanimity, agreement, proposal of love
clematis	mental beauty		
columbine	resolution		
cornflower	delicacy	primrose	early youth
daffodil	regard and chivalry	rose	love
dahlia	good taste	rosemary	remembrance, your presence revives me
daisy	innocence		
dogwood	durability	sweet basil	good wishes
gladiola	strong character	sweet pea	delicate pleasures, lasting pleasures
heliotrope	devotion		
honeysuckle	devoted affection, bonds of love	sweet william	gallantry
		tulip, yellow	hopeless love
hyacinth	sport, game, play	violet	faithfulness
hydrangea	heartlessness	zinnia	thoughts of an absent friend
lilac	youthful innocence		
morning glory	affection		

Flowers leave some of their fragrance
in the hand that bestows them.

Chinese Proverb

A Time for Sharing

Gardening with Open Arms

t's an ancient rhythm, dependable since the dawn of history.

"While the earth remaineth," was the promise, "seedtime and harvest, and cold and heat, and summer and winter, and day and night shall not cease."

And they don't. Year after year the days and the seasons and seedtime and harvest continue apace, right in my own backyard. And as a gardener I am privileged to participate in the process.

I play favorites with the age-old rhythm, though.

I like seedtime fine. And I really do enjoy the unfolding of the garden through the successive days and nights.

But what I really love best is the harvest.

It is my greatest joy to go out on our property and bring in an apron load of lemons, avocados, nectarines...or a basket of roses and lilies and some exuberant parsley and fragrant rosemary. I love to see the produce heaped in the bowl on my kitchen table, love to snip the basil directly into my tomato sauce, love to gather an armload of daisies and zinnias to make a bouquet.

It feels like Christmas, like the garden has given me a gift.

And it has, of course.

Every day my garden lavishes on me gifts of beauty and serenity and wonderful fragrance and succulent flavor.

My response is to say thank you, every single day. I want to keep remembering that all this is a gift. Even after I have worked to help bring it about, it's still a gift.

And then I have another response.

I want to share.

The main reason I love to share my garden is that sharing multiplies my joy.

Bob and I bought our property in the first place with sharing in mind. We have plenty of room for conferences and open houses and for overnight guests. We love to barbecue out in the garden, or just to have people over for tea and talk. And every time I look at my garden through the eyes of a visitor, I receive its gifts anew.

I'm far from the first person to discover this open secret about sharing. So many of the gardeners I know are openhearted sharers. They love to lavish the people around them with cuttings and bouquets and tomatoes and stories about their gardens.

I know of one gentlemen, a retired professor in Tennessee, who raises roses as a hobby and shares them as an avocation. As soon as the blossoms begin appearing in the spring, he begins his rounds, bringing fresh blooms to the office of his church and to his son-in-law's place of business. Every day from May until September, every desk in both of those offices is graced by a single fresh bloom. Keeping his church and the business in roses is one of his greatest joys.

> Flowers and fruits are always fit presents,—flowers, because they are a proud assertion that a ray of beauty outvalues all the utilities of the world.
>
> RALPH
> WALDO
> EMERSON

That gentleman is well aware that being able to give is one of the most valuable privileges of living—a privilege we sometimes don't miss until it's withdrawn.

A friend of a friend, just out of college, has taken a job providing home care for senior citizens. Her job is go to their homes, help them bathe, mop their kitchens—do whatever they need to be able to continue living on their own. She finds the work deeply satisfying, but she is frustrated by one of the rules of her employment: She is not allowed to accept meals or any other gifts from her clients.

Why is this frustrating? Simply because the elderly women she works with are constantly offering to cook for her, to feed her, and she feels their deep hurt when she has to refuse. Occasionally she chooses to bend the rules so that they can have the joy of giving to her.

Giving is the source of some of life's deepest satisfactions, and even the simplest garden can provide us with so many opportu-nities to share with others.

The most obvious gift, of course, is the bouquet. Remember the joy of running to your mother with your chubby fist full of wildflowers? Our grandchildren love to gather bouquets from our garden for the dinner table, for their mothers and teachers, and for me, too. And Bob is always coming in from his outdoor work with a little love offering: a fresh handful of our Valentine sweet peas, a single lily, even some leafy branches he trimmed off a shrub. No matter the flower or the size, these simple gifts always warm my heart.

I think we need far more flower giving in this country. Europeans have long had the custom of bringing flowers whenever they are invited to someone's house to visit. Wouldn't it be wonderful if this charming custom was adopted in the United States—especially with inexpensive flowers so readily available in supermarkets and even convenience stores. And how much nicer to present the gift of a bouquet from your very own garden!

The gifts of the garden readily lend themselves to handcrafted offerings. Dried flowers and herbs can be fashioned into lovely wreaths. Pressed flowers and herbs adorn note cards and pictures and wall hangings. Herbs and vegetables contribute to delectable homemade dishes or shine in simple baskets of fresh produce. And don't forget cross-stitch or needlepoint pictures in garden themes.

If your garden includes vegetables, you are probably already familiar with the joy of giving—and perhaps the frustration of trying to give, since for most harvests are too bountiful for one family. Perhaps you have even encountered the challenge of offering bushels of tomatoes or zucchini or onions to neighbors and coworkers who have their own gardens. Sometimes these vegetables seem to multiply even after they are off the vines.

I do urge you to consider ways you can offer your surplus to provide precious food for the hungry. Nearly every town has some sort of food pantry that will accept fruits and vegetables and distribute them to people in need. Soup kitchens can also make practical and charitable use of your vegetables and would probably welcome gifts of fresh herbs as well. Why not grow extra next year and offer to spend time working in the soup kitchen? And don't forget that it's important to feed the soul as well as the body. Perhaps you can offer bouquets for the tables—maybe simple nose-gays in soda-bottle vases with cheerful ribbons.

And don't forget that people in need of the gifts from your garden may be under your very own nose. You may think you don't know any truly hungry people. But is your neighbor's son in graduate school,

> Is there any sense to the notion that a person has to know a subject from A to Z in order to begin teaching it effectively? If you are sure of your ground as far as you have gone, if you know the alphabet to M, let us say, you can teach that much of it, can't you?... Following up that theory, in my third year of gardening I began to teach it. Next to working in my own garden I like starting one for somebody else.
>
> **R U T H S T O U T**

trying to live on a scholarship and a part-time income? He may welcome the gift of salad greens and the makings for zucchini lasagna. Does your church know of shut-ins who could use a meal of fresh-cooked vegetables and a hand-picked bouquet? And what about the elderly woman up the block who waves when you and your children walk by? Are you sure she's eating well?

From these very basic ideas, a million possibilities start to gather. I have found that my garden is a bountiful resource for gifts of all kinds.

A little basket of potpourri makes a thoughtful housewarming gift.

A preplanted herb garden with recipes or bottles of home-dried herbs will delight a newlywed cook.

An airplane plant made by potting one of the "babies" from your hanging basket can be a treat for a friend in the hospital.

A big bouquet and a packet of seeds proclaims a warm welcome to a new family to the neighborhood.

With imagination and a few basic skills, your garden becomes a cornucopia of gifts for every season. But garden gifts can encompass so much more than the fruits of a particular garden.

You can also give the gift of the garden itself.

Bob and I like to keep our garden gate open so that friends and neighbors can enjoy the trees and flowers. The nice thing about garden work is that you can stop to say hello and to chat awhile and then resume the task at hand. We have found that many of our guests can entertain themselves in our garden—it's a treat just to wander over by the fish pond and sit.

Other guests relish the chance to pitch in, and we don't hesitate to hand a houseguest a spade or a watering can. While we would never trap a casual visitor into doing heavy work like turning sod, and we don't really turn colleagues in their business suits out to weed the radishes, we do open our garden to participation. A friend who drops by in blue jeans may well get the chance to pick grapefruit.

Yet another way you can give the gift of your garden is by volunteering your labor and expertise. You might help an older relative hoe or plant and gain a basketful of helpful tips in return. Or if you're an experienced gardener, you might ask the novice down the street if there is any way you can help. Give gifts of cuttings from your own plants, seeds you have collected, even extra tools. And don't forget the gift of your encouragement.

Finally, there are gifts *for* the garden, gifts for the gardener. Just a little experience working with plants and flowers will suggest items a beginning or experienced gardener would appreciate. Pruners and shears are always welcome, as are garden books. Why not trim a sun hat or a visor for the gardener to wear on the job? Use a glue gun to attach ribbon, silk flowers, or even a bow fashioned from garden gloves. Garden stores and mail-order catalogs are full of items to make a lovely garden even lovelier—from whimsical row markers to birdhouses to bubbling fountains. And there's nothing to warm a gardener's heart like a gift certificate to a garden-supply store or a favorite seed catalog.

You may find, of course, that this kind of shopping begins to warm your own heart, to inspire dreams not of what you want to give to others, but what you want to do next in your own garden.

Perhaps you spot a new variety of daylily, a new color of phlox, a colorful wildflower mix. Perhaps. . .

Give in to the temptation.

All you'll really be doing is investing in the gifts of the future.

Time did truly begin in a garden—a garden filled with lush vegetation, food for every creature. With just a little of your own time you can enjoy the gift of your own garden—and spend your days and hours surrounded by the awesome and giving hand of nature.

A Giver's Supply Cabinet

Materials to Have on Hand for Impromptu Gifts

If you set up all your supplies in one place, you'll be all set to create a garden gift at a moment's notice!

- sharp scissors and pruners
- nonmetallic bucket for conditioning flowers
- flower-gathering basket or "trug" long enough to hold long-stemmed flowers lying down
- cut flower preservative
- assorted vases, bowls, and containers
- baskets—all sizes, including miniature
- plastic pots saved from purchased plants—to cover with fabric or plant with leftover seedlings to grow and use as gifts
- chicken wire for scrunching into the necks of large vases (tape in place) or covering blocks of floral foam for topiary
- green florist wire to support floppy flowers
- floral clay to hold arrangements in place
- floral foam to absorb water and hold flowers in place
- florist's tape to hold arrangements in place in containers
- dental floss or clear fishing line to tie flowers and foliage to wreaths or to garlands
- plastic flower tubes to hold single flowers or several thin-stemmed ones for arranging
- decorator moss to cover bare soil or glue onto baskets, plastic containers, wreaths
- Spanish moss—long silver-gray strands to hide soil or use as filler in wreaths
- quick-dry liquid cement or tacky craft glue
- glue gun and glue sticks
- craft scissors
- assorted ribbons—very thin to six inches wide
- plain gift cards to decorate with fresh, dried, or pressed flowers and attach to gifts
- clear plastic self-adhesive paper for attaching pressed flowers and leaves to glass, note cards, stationery
- assortment of pens and markers

> Were there no God, we would be in this glorious world with grateful hearts and no one to thank.
>
> **CHRISTINA ROSSETTI**

Plant a Row for the Hungry

Here's a creative and exciting idea for sharing the bounty of your garden. Dubbed Plant a Row for the Hungry, it's a plan that's beginning to spread throughout the country.

The idea is simple: Anyone who plants a vegetable garden simply plants an additional row for sharing. Most gardeners can find the space, and the extra row doesn't represent that much extra work, but it can yield remarkable results in terms of getting fresh food to people who need it.

One of the beauties of the Plant a Row for the Hungry idea is its flexibility. Gardeners can work with a local food program or even a national program such as Second Harvest (1-800-532-3663). Or a group of gardeners in one neighborhood could band together informally to supply elderly neighbors or single parents with shared food. The possibilities are endless, the satisfactions profound. Can you think of a spot for your extra row?

A Basket of Bounty

Creating Gifts from Your Garden

I've always enjoyed giving gift baskets. Somehow a collection of small gifts in a pretty basket with a bow seems like so much more gift for the money! But these garden gift-basket ideas are actually quite inexpensive, especially if you include the bounty from your own garden. Try these gift basket ideas, or use your imagination to create your own.

• **THE BEGINNER:** Fill the basket with gardening essentials and amenities: hand tools, an apron, a how-to book suited for the recipient's region, and a pretty potted plant grown from your own cuttings. Wire a set of gardening gloves to the basket handle in the middle and spread the fingers and wrists out to make a bow. Then tuck in a homemade gift certificate for help and advice.

• **THE WINTER GARDENER:** For a winter gardener beginning to feel cabin fever, give the gift of a garden journal, some garden magazines, and a book of quotations about the garden. In the midst of these publications, tuck a potted narcissus or amaryllis bulb with instructions on how to grow indoors. Tie on a big green bow with a decorative pen wired on to it. Another idea is to add in a gift certificate from the garden center.

• **THE FLOWER GATHERER:** Long "trug" basket that long-stemmed flowers can lie in. Add clipping shears, a couple of "finds" from the antique market for vases, a book on flower

arranging, florist wire and tape, and half a dozen packets of commercial floral preservative. Attach a big bow and a bunch of fresh, dried, or silk flowers. You can also decorate a plastic bucket for your container.

• **THE BIRDER:** If you can find some bird-printed fabric, use that to line your basket. Tuck in a small bird feeder, a bag of wild bird seed, and a field guide for identifying birds in your area. Tie on a matching bow along with a cuttlebone from the pet store.

• **THE CANNER:** Fill a round basket with an assortment of your favorite jams, jellies, and relishes. Tuck a set of pretty napkins or dishtowels around the dishes and add a little rubber ring for opening the cans.

• **THE SALAD LOVER:** Line basket with small garden-print tablecloth or picnic cloth. (You can make your own from garden-print fabric.) Then add Ziploc bags holding fresh lettuces, a little red cabbage, a couple of tomatoes and cucumbers, a head of garlic, and a little bottle of your favorite herbs. Small bottles of extra-virgin olive oil and herb vinegar are also nice, or tuck in a loaf of Parmesan Dill Bread and pot of Healthy Herbed Butter Spread (see recipes pages 46 and 47).

• **PASTA PERFECT:** In a long basket pack fresh tomatoes, basil, garlic, and a little bottle of olive oil. Tie a bundle of whole-wheat spaghetti with red, green, and white ribbons and add Italian Bread, herbed butter, and a shaker of Parmesan. Don't forget to tuck in the recipe for Emilie's Fresh Tomato Pasta Sauce (see page 45). Mama Mia!

• **FOR THE BATH:** Line a small basket with a pretty set of face towels or washcloths. Tuck in a bottle ~~~~ ath and a half dozen Roses upon Roses Bath Sachets (see chapter 3). Include a little card ~~~~ heir use.

• **SWEET DREAMS:** Buy a set of embroidered pillowcases to line edges of basket. Stitch up a dream pillow as shown in chapter 3 and add a card explaining what to do with it. Surround the pillow with a dozen little sachets made out of lace handkerchiefs or other pretty, feminine fabric. You can also add a sleep mask, a lullaby tape, or even a negligee. Tie with a big pink bow.

• **THE HERB PLANTER:** Thoroughly wash a large clay pot with vinegar water and let dry. Use acrylic paint to decorate the outside of the pot and the inside rim. Spray with varnish. When dry, add a bag of potting soil, packets of herb seeds suitable to plant together, marigold seeds to surround the outside, a small trowel, and a book on growing and using herbs.

• **THE HERB CHEF:** Line a basket with bright dish towels. Buy five or six small plastic bags from a craft store or pick up some spice bottles from a cooking supply shop. Fill with your home-dried herbs (see recipes in chapter 2) and label each. Add bottled spices and basic sauces, some recipes or a cookbook, and a cooking mitt. A great gift for a newlywed—collecting an herb collection is expensive.

For flowers that bloom about our feet,

Father, we thank Thee;

For tender grass so fresh and sweet,

Father, we thank Thee.

For the song of bird and hum of bee,

For all things fair we hear or see,

Father in heaven, we thank Thee.

Ralph Waldo Emerson